HEALING YOUR INNER CHILD WORKBOOK

—— 5 IN 1 ——

The Complete 5-Part Blueprint to Heal Wounds, Reparent Yourself, and Break Free from Trauma Forever

VIVIAN WHITMORE

© **Copyright 2025 - All rights reserved.**

The contents of this book may not be reproduced, duplicated or transmitted without direct written permission from the author.

Under no circumstances will any legal responsibility or blame be held against the publisher for any reparation, damages, or monetary loss due to the information herein, either directly or indirectly.

Legal Notice:
You cannot amend, distribute, sell, use, quote or paraphrase any part of the content within this book without the consent of the author.

Disclaimer Notice:
Please note the information contained within this document is for educational and entertainment purposes only. No warranties of any kind are expressed or implied. Readers acknowledge that the author is not engaging in the rendering of legal, financial, medical or professional advice.

CONTENTS

BOOK 1: Inner Child Healing—A Comprehensive Workbook to Understand Your Emotional Triggers and Begin the Journey to Inner Peace

Introduction -- 9
Chapter 1: What Is the Inner Child? -- 11
Chapter 2: Identifying Emotional Triggers Rooted in Childhood --------- 20
Chapter 3: The Impact of Early Experiences on Adult Life ----------------- 31
Chapter 4: Awareness and Recognition in Healing ------------------------- 41
Chapter 5: Recognizing the Need for Inner Child Healing ----------------- 49
Conclusion -- 60

BOOK 2: Inner Child Reparenting—Practical Tools to Build Emotional Strength, Set Boundaries, and Foster Self-Compassion

Introduction -- 63
Chapter 1: The Basics of Reparenting Your Inner Child -------------------- 65
Chapter 2: Developing Emotional Resilience and Self-Love -------------- 70
Chapter 3: Setting and Maintaining Healthy Boundaries ------------------ 82
Chapter 4: Practicing Self-Soothing Techniques ----------------------------- 89
Chapter 5: Creating a Safe Emotional Environment ----------------------- 101
Conclusion --- 109

BOOK 3: Emotional Healing Workbook— Step-by-Step Guidance to Release Pain, Overcome Self-Sabotage, and Find Lasting Freedom

Introduction --- 113
Chapter 1: Processing Painful Childhood Memories ----------------------- 115
Chapter 2: Techniques for Letting Go of Guilt, Shame and Resentment - 125
Chapter 3: Understanding and Overcoming Self-Sabotaging Behaviors - 137
Chapter 4: Rewriting Limiting Beliefs Rooted in Childhood --------------- 146
Chapter 5: Building Emotional Freedom and Peace ------------------------ 156
Conclusion --- 166

BOOK 4: Inner Child Relationships—Break Negative Patterns, Improve Communication, and Build Authentic Connections

Introduction --- 169
Chapter 1: The Link Between Childhood Trauma and Relationship Patterns -- 171
Chapter 2: Recognizing and Breaking Free from Toxic Dynamics --------- 181
Chapter 3: Trusting and Communicating Effectively ---------------------- 190
Chapter 4: Encouraging Emotional Vulnerability and Authentic Connections -- 198
Chapter 5: Building Strong, Healthy Relationships ---------------------- 214
Conclusion -- 225

BOOK 5: Authentic Self Workbook—Transform Your Life with Daily Practices to Embrace Confidence, Joy, and Inner Fulfillment

Introduction --- 229
Chapter 1: Rediscovering Your Authentic Self After Healing -------------- 231
Chapter 2: Cultivating Daily Practices for Self-Love and Confidence ----- 240
Chapter 3: Embracing Joy and Playfulness in Everyday Life -------------- 251
Chapter 4: Sustaining Inner Peace Through Personal Growth ------------- 264
Chapter 5: The Ongoing Journey to Wholeness--------------------------- 280
Conclusion -- 292

INTRODUCTION

As I sat on the edge of my bed, surrounded by a sea of scattered papers and colored pencils, I stumbled upon an old box filled with mementos from my childhood. Each item, from the crayon drawings to the faded photographs, was a gateway to a world I had left behind.

At that moment, I was flooded with memories—some joyful and others tinged with sadness. It was as if my inner child were inviting me to revisit the emotions and experiences that shaped who I am today. This encounter inspired me to begin a journey of healing and self-discovery, and I wish to share the lessons I have learned from this path.

In an ever-evolving world, pursuing emotional well-being and personal growth is more important than ever, especially if you grapple with unresolved childhood wounds.

The *Healing Your Inner Child Workbook 5-in-1* series is a comprehensive resource for those seeking to address their emotional struggles and reclaim their future through life-changing self-help strategies. This unique collection consolidates five distinct yet interconnected workbooks, offering a holistic approach to inner child recovery and emotional growth.

These workbooks aim to merge theory with practical exercises, fostering a deep insight into emotional patterns and providing actionable tools for self-healing. Each workbook begins with the foundational elements that guide you in recognizing and understanding your emotional triggers, leading into chapters filled with practical exercises to facilitate healing and personal growth. The content is structured to encourage introspection and self-discovery, prompting you to engage actively with your emotions and past experiences.

The series focuses on five key areas, each addressing a specific facet of inner child work:

- ❏ **Inner Child Healing:** Exploring emotional triggers and understanding the impact of childhood experiences on adult life.

- ❏ **Inner Child Reparenting:** Equipping you with practical tools to nurture your inner child, set healthy boundaries, and practice self-compassion.

- ❑ **Emotional Healing:** Offering step-by-step guidance to help you process painful memories, overcome self-sabotage, and find lasting freedom.

- ❑ **Inner Child Relationships:** Analyzing how childhood wounds affect relationships and providing strategies to create healthier connections.

- ❑ **Authentic Self:** Empowering you to reconnect with your true self and cultivate joy, confidence, and inner fulfillment.

Working through these workbooks will empower you to confront and heal from your past, breaking free from repetitive patterns that hinder your emotional well-being. Each workbook concludes with reflective exercises summarizing key insights, paving the way for continued personal growth in subsequent volumes.

This series is helpful for a diverse audience, including young adults seeking to resolve early life challenges, middle-aged individuals focused on breaking generational cycles, mental health professionals looking for additional resources, trauma survivors seeking self-guided healing, and emotionally introspective individuals aiming for a fulfilling second half of life.

Healing Your Inner Child Workbook 5 in 1 invites you to take charge of your healing journey. Whether you are beginning your path to emotional recovery or strengthening your understanding of inner child work, these workbooks provide invaluable resources for promoting emotional resilience, building healthier relationships, and embracing a life rich with joy and self-acceptance.

Your journey begins here, and the possibilities are boundless.

BOOK 1

Inner Child Healing

A Comprehensive Workbook to Understand Your Emotional Triggers and Begin the Journey to Inner Peace

INTRODUCTION

Welcome to Inner Child Healing: A Comprehensive Workbook to Understand Your Emotional Triggers and Begin the Journey to Inner Peace. This workbook serves as the foundational entry point into the life-changing world of inner child work, offering you the tools and insights to start your journey of self-discovery and emotional healing.

At the heart of this workbook lies the concept of the inner child—a representation of your childhood experiences, emotions, and memories. Understanding your inner child is essential for recognizing how past events shape your current emotional responses and behaviors.

In this workbook, you will explore these triggers and become aware of their important role in your emotional landscape. Through engaging theoretical insights and practical exercises, you will learn to identify and reconnect with this essential aspect of yourself.

The key chapters systematically guide you through the process of healing:

- **What Is the Inner Child?**
- **Identifying Emotional Triggers Rooted in Childhood**
- **The Impact of Early Experiences on Adult Life**
- **Creating Awareness of Emotional Patterns**
- **Recognizing the Need for Inner Child Healing**

To begin with, we will explore the emotional triggers rooted in childhood. You will gain clarity on how these triggers influence your reactions and relationships in adulthood. As we spotlight these triggers, you can acquire awareness and break free from the unhelpful patterns that may have held you back for years.

We will also examine the impact of early experiences on adulthood, helping you understand the connections between your past and present. Journaling prompts and emotional mapping exercises will allow you to reflect on your personal history and its importance in shaping who you are today. We designed these activities to provide you with a structured way to explore your emotional landscape, offering insights that can lead to meaningful healing.

This workbook emphasizes the importance of recognizing emotional patterns. By recognizing the recurring themes in your life, you can identify the emotional wounds begging for attention.

Each chapter will incorporate reflection activities that allow you to assess how these past experiences manifest in your current behaviors and relationships. This self-reflective process is key to understanding the need for inner child healing and empowering you to take the next steps in your journey.

As you progress through this workbook, remember that healing takes time and patience. Each exercise is crafted to facilitate gentle exploration without overwhelming you. Embrace this journey of self-discovery with an open heart and mind, knowing that you are not alone in this process. Allow yourself to feel, process, and heal as you uncover the layers of your inner child.

By the end of this workbook, you will have laid a strong foundation for your healing journey, equipping you with the knowledge and tools to foster inner peace.

Let's begin this life-changing adventure together, unlocking the path to emotional wholeness and a more fulfilling life.

CHAPTER 1:

What Is the Inner Child?

Are you struggling to gain control of your life? You may have heard the term "inner child" and are curious about it. Your inner child represents the youthful aspects of your personality that hold emotions and memories from your formative years. Throughout this chapter, we'll explore the origins of certain emotional responses and encourage gentle self-reflection.

Quick Check-In Exercise

Before we begin exploring your inner child, take a moment to check in with yourself:

Rate your current level (1–10):

- ❑ Understanding of the inner child concept: _____
- ❑ Connection with your childhood memories: _____
- ❑ Comfort with emotional exploration: _____

What brings you to inner child work today?
_____

What do you hope to gain from this exploration?
_____
_____
_____
_____

Definition And Importance Of The Inner Child

Your inner child represents the youthful aspects of your personality that hold emotions and memories from your formative years (Goldstein, n.d.).

Although distant, exploring childhood reconnects you with an essential aspect of yourself. Neglecting this part of your inner world may lead to missed insights about your behavior and emotional triggers.

For example, if you felt abandoned when you were younger, you might react strongly to situations that remind you of that time. As you come to understand these patterns, you can begin to heal and become more self-aware, which helps you figure out why certain things upset you. Understanding how these childhood experiences influence your present enables your healing and personal growth.

Interactive Exercise

To get started, write about a childhood memory where you felt unseen. Reflect on how that experience affects you today. This exercise will set the stage for your journey into healing and self-discovery.

_____

_____

In relationships, knowing how your inner child impacts you can improve communication and empathy. Understanding each partner's childhood issues can help resolve conflicts. This sensitive approach reduces defensiveness and builds trust, turning fights into chances for growth and strengthening your connections.

Many of the ways adults cope with problems are defense mechanisms formed in childhood. While these methods may have helped back then, they can hold you back now. Looking back at these habits, you can learn to let them go and adopt better tools like mindfulness and cognitive-behavioral techniques. Reconnecting with your inner child promotes self-compassion and helps you grow through reflection and creativity.

Cultural And Historical Perspectives

Different cultures perceive the inner child variably, offering diverse healing approaches. Indigenous cultures may connect this concept to spiritual practices for holistic wellness, while Eastern philosophies emphasize harmonizing energies for personal balance. These perspectives promote emotional flexibility and encourage individuals to adopt various strategies for nurturing emotional health.

The inner child concept has a rich historical foundation in psychological theories, notably Carl Jung's "eternal child" archetype, which represents the youthfulness within us throughout life (Meet Your Inner Child, 2024). This understanding legitimizes personal experiences, framing struggles as part of a shared human journey.

Getting To Know Your Inner Child: Practical Exercises

Exploring your inner child can lead to healing and self-discovery, allowing you to reconnect with the joy, creativity, and curiosity that reside within you.

Exercise 1: Meeting Your Inner Child

Close your eyes and imagine yourself as a child. What age comes to mind first?

- ❏ Age that appeared: _____
- ❏ What were you wearing? _____
- ❏ Where were you? _____
- ❏ What emotions came up? _____

Exercise 2: Childhood Safe Place

Create a safe space for your inner child:

- ❏ Describe a place where you felt safe as a child: _____
- ❏ What made it feel safe? _____
- ❏ What activities did you enjoy there? _____
- ❏ Who (if anyone) was with you? _____

Exercise 3: Creative Expression

Choose one:

- ❏ Draw your inner child.

- ❑ Write a letter to your inner child.
- ❑ Create a collage representing your childhood.
- ❑ Make a playlist of songs from your childhood.

Use this space to create or reflect on your chosen activity:

_____

_____

_____

Exercise 4: Childhood Memory Box

Create a physical connection to your inner child:

- ❑ Find a special box or container
- ❑ Gather five items from your childhood (or representations of them)
- ❑ For each item, complete:

Item	Why it's special	Feeling it brings up

Exercise 5: Inner Child Time Machine

If you could spend one hour with yourself as a child:

- ❑ What age would you choose? _____
- ❑ Where would you go? _____
- ❑ What would you do together? _____
- ❑ What would you say? _____

MORE PRACTICAL EXERCISES

These exercises encourage introspection and self-discovery, helping you understand your inner child's influence on your emotional landscape while laying the groundwork for healing and personal growth. Don't feel pressured to complete them all at once; doing so may become emotionally draining, so you should take it one step at a time.

Journaling Prompts

Prompt 1: Reflect on a Recent Experience

Reflect on a recent experience where you felt an overwhelming emotional reaction (like anger, sadness, anxiety). Write about the incident in detail:

- ❑ What emotions did you feel at that moment?
- ❑ Can you trace these feelings back to any childhood experiences?
- ❑ Consider how this awareness might shift your understanding of the situation.

_____

_____

_____

Prompt 2: Create a List

Create a list of situations that consistently trigger strong emotions. For each, identify the emotions that arise and the childhood memories associated with these triggers. Reflect on what these reveal about your past and how they might influence your present behavior.

_____

_____

_____

_____

Prompt 3: Thinking About Experiences

Think about when you felt misunderstood or unsupported as a child. How does this experience affect your emotional reactions in similar situations today? Recognizing these connections promotes self-compassion and promotes healing.

_____

_____

_____

Prompt 4: Identify a Current Relationship

Identify a current relationship that feels challenging.

❑ What emotions surface when engaging with this person?

❑ How might your inner child's experiences contribute to these feelings?

Explore ways to communicate these insights to the other person to foster understanding.

_____

_____

_____

Emotional Mapping Exercises

Activity: Create an Inner Child Map

1) In the center of a blank page, write "Inner Child" and draw a circle around it.

2) Branch out with lines to different qualities or characteristics of your inner child (like joy, creativity, playfulness, fear, insecurity).

3) For each quality, branch out to:

   a) specific childhood memories that embody those qualities.

   b) current situations where you notice these qualities emerging or being suppressed.

4) Review your map. Look for patterns: How do these aspects of your inner child shape your daily life and interactions? What insights can you glean about the needs and desires of your inner child that may be influencing your adult behavior?

_____
_____
_____

Reflective Activities

Activity 1: Reflective Narrative

Select a childhood memory that continues to influence you. Describe the people involved, the events, and your feelings. Analyze its impact on your adult behaviors and reactions, identifying patterns. Reflect on how understanding this memory can assist in your personal healing journey.

_____
_____
_____

Activity 2: Inner Child Dialogue

Write a dialogue between your adult self and your inner child. Ask your inner child how they feel about past experiences and what they wish to express. Respond with compassion and understanding, reflecting on how this interaction shapes your perception of their needs.

_____
_____
_____
_____

Activity 3: Behavioral Reflection

Identify a behavior you want to change, like avoiding conflict or seeking approval. Reflect on the first instance of this behavior and your feelings. Analyze its connection to your inner child and past wounds. Acknowledging this can guide your approach to change and help you develop healthier responses.

_____

_____

_____

This inner child exploration has internal and external benefits like enhanced empathy and communication, as well as improved relationships. It develops emotional awareness, healthier coping strategies, and resilience. Inner child healing develops self-compassion, leading to a fulfilled and peaceful existence.

LOOKING AHEAD

As you work through these exercises, notice how your relationship with your inner child evolves. In the next chapter, we'll explore identifying emotional triggers rooted in childhood.

Final Reflection

What's your key takeaway from this chapter?

_____

_____

_____

What practice will you start with tomorrow?

_____

_____

_____

Your Personal Notes

Use this space for additional thoughts and insights:

CHAPTER 2:

Identifying Emotional Triggers Rooted in Childhood

Have you ever thought about why certain situations make you feel emotions you didn't expect? Do you struggle with anxiety or fear that seems to come out of nowhere? Understanding the emotional triggers from your childhood can lead to important insights and personal growth.

These hidden influences affect how you react as an adult, even if the connections are not obvious. Identifying and dealing with these triggers can help you understand your emotional responses and encourage healing.

Quick Check-In Exercise

Before we explore your emotional triggers, take a moment to check in with yourself:

Rate your current level (1–10):

- ❑ Awareness of your emotional triggers: _____

- ❑ Understanding of your reactions: _____

- ❑ Comfort with exploring past experiences: _____

What makes you most reactive emotionally?

_____

What patterns would you like to change?

_____

_____

Understanding Emotional Triggers

What Are Emotional Triggers?

Emotional triggers are stimuli that evoke intense emotional reactions seemingly disproportionate to the present situation. These triggers often originate in childhood experiences, when our brains formed patterns to protect us from perceived threats or to cope with our environment.

Signs of Unresolved Childhood Triggers

- ❑ intense reactions to minor situations
- ❑ recurring relationship patterns
- ❑ persistent avoidance behaviors
- ❑ physical manifestations of emotional pain
- ❑ social anxiety and self-doubt

Emotional Trigger Tracking Worksheet

Instructions

Record instances when you experience strong emotional reactions that seem disproportionate to the situation. Complete this worksheet daily for at least one week.

Daily Entry

Date:_____

Topic	Questions	Answers
Situation	What happened? Be specific about circumstances, people involved, and what was said or done.	
Emotional response	What emotions did you feel? (anger, fear, shame, sadness, and more.)	
Intensity (1–10)	How intense was it?	

Topic	Questions	Answers
Physical sensations	What did you notice in your body? (like tension, racing heart, nausea.)	
Thoughts	What thoughts went through your mind?	
Possible childhood connection	Does this remind you of any childhood experience?	

Reflection Questions

1) Do you notice any patterns in what triggers strong emotional responses?

2) How might these triggers connect to your childhood experiences?

3) What needs might be going unmet in these moments?

4) What would help you respond differently next time?

_____

_____

_____

Weekly Review

After tracking for one week, answer these questions:

1) What common triggers did you identify?

2) Which childhood experiences seem most connected to your current triggers?

3) What healthy coping strategies could you implement when triggered?

4) What boundaries might you need to set to protect yourself?

5) Are there specific relationships or situations that consistently trigger you?

_____

_____

Tips for Identifying Childhood Connections

- ❑ Notice if your reaction feels familiar from earlier in life.
- ❑ Consider if your emotional response matches the intensity of the situation.
- ❑ Reflect on whether you're responding to the present moment or to past hurts.
- ❑ Look for recurring themes across different triggering situations.
- ❑ Pay attention to your body's response—it often remembers what the mind forgets.

Signs Of Unresolved Childhood Triggers

When examining intense emotional reactions to seemingly minor triggers, you should try to pinpoint what happened in your past that triggered this. Now that you've begun tracking your triggers, let's explore how different childhood experiences might shape your adult emotional responses.

Pay Attention to Unusual Emotional Responses

To find emotional triggers from childhood, pay attention to situations that cause strong emotional reactions. Keeping a journal can help. Whenever you feel a strong reaction, write down what happened and any feelings or memories that come up. You may see patterns that link to childhood events or needs that were not met. This process helps you become more aware and allows you to take steps toward healing.

Recurring Unhealthy Relationship Patterns

These patterns mirror your unmet childhood needs. For example, being frequently attracted to emotionally unavailable partners may reflect a lack of emotional support in your past. Recognizing these patterns is the first step toward change. Acknowledging them allows you to begin to challenge and alter these dynamics, seeking healthier relationships that fulfill your present needs.

To break free from these patterns, recognize how early relationships shape your expectations. Consider therapy for deeper insights and to develop healthier relationship skills. Practice mindfulness to become aware of these patterns in your daily life and actively choose different responses. Engage in supportive communities where you can learn from others with similar experiences.

Avoidance Behaviors as a Result of Childhood

Avoiding conflict might stem from growing up in a household where arguments lead to severe repercussions. Such avoidance impedes emotional growth and prevents addressing core issues. The key to changing avoidance into engagement is gradually confronting feared situations in safe and controlled environments. It's about building resilience and learning that facing discomfort leads to strength and healing.

To tackle avoidance, start by gently exposing yourself to the situations you fear most, incrementing the intensity as you grow more comfortable. Self-reflection is important; asking yourself questions about the origin of these fears can illuminate their roots.

Engaging in supportive exercises like guided visualizations or cognitive behavioral techniques will aid in dismantling avoidance mechanisms.

Emotional Pain Stored in Your Body

Physical symptoms like chronic stress often manifest unaddressed emotional pain, underscoring the complex mind-body connection. The body can store emotional pain from unresolved childhood issues, resulting in ailments such as tension headaches, digestive problems, or unexplained fatigue. Stress, in particular, is a common manifestation of hidden emotional turmoil.

Exploring this connection involves paying close attention to physical symptoms and considering possible emotional underpinnings. For instance, persistent stomach aches might not just be dietary issues but could relate to anxiety stemming from early abandonment fears. Consider following a holistic approach that combines traditional medical treatments with psychological interventions for optimal results.

Self-awareness regarding physical manifestations includes identifying stressors linked to emotional triggers. Practices like yoga, meditation, or regular exercise help alleviate physical stress while promoting mental clarity.

How will you know if you are experiencing physical manifestations? Seek professional guidance to decode and correlate your bodily signals with potential emotional triggers.

Exploring alternative therapies such as acupuncture or massage can also help release stored tension, offering relief and promoting healing.

Childhood Trauma and Sensitivity

Traumatic experiences create heightened sensitivity to similar situations. For instance, if you experienced loss early in life, you might respond with intense anxiety to potential separation from loved ones.

Quick Exercise

List three situations that consistently provoke strong emotional reactions. Can you identify any childhood experiences that might be connected?

_____

_____

_____

Social Interactions and Self-Perception

Your childhood social experiences shaped how you perceive yourself in groups. Consider:

- ❏ Were you included or excluded by peers?
- ❏ How did you handle conflict with friends?
- ❏ Did you feel valued in social settings?

Quick Exercise

Notice your emotional responses in your next three social interactions. Journal about any connections to childhood social experiences.

_____

_____

_____

The Part Childhood Role Models Play

The role models and behaviors observed during childhood serve as unwritten guides that shape our adult choices and habits. Children naturally emulate the adults around them, absorbing values and behaviors that seem normal within their familial context. Positive role models can instill virtues such as empathy, kindness, and perseverance, creating similarly healthy behaviors in adulthood. If childhood role models exhibited detrimental behaviors—like dishonesty or excessive criticism—these can also become ingrained and surface in adult interactions and decision-making processes.

To counteract this influence, you must reflect on the qualities they admired or resented in their childhood role models. This reflection allows for more intentional choices, allowing individuals to decide which behaviors they wish to emulate or change consciously. Thus, it helps foster more informed and deliberate decisions in their personal and professional lives.

Recognizing and addressing these dysfunctional patterns can pave the way to healthier relationships and a more fulfilling life.

More Practical Exercises

Explore a variety of engaging exercises designed for you to break free from your emotional triggers.

Exposure Practice for Avoidance Behaviors

If you notice yourself avoiding certain situations due to childhood fears:

1) Create a "fear ladder"—list situations from least to most scary.

2) Start with the least intimidating scenario.

3) Practice gradual exposure with self-compassion.

4) Celebrate each step forward, no matter how small.

_____

_____

_____

Journaling Prompts

Prompt 1: Reflect on a Recent Situation

Reflect on a recent situation in which you had a strong emotional response that seemed excessive for what occurred. Describe the event and your feelings in detail. How might this reaction connect to specific childhood memories or unmet needs from your past?

_____

_____

_____

Prompt 2: Reflect on Your Relationships

Reflect on your relationships with your parents or primary caregivers during childhood. What messages did you receive about love, trust, and self-worth? Write about how these early messages impact your current emotional responses and the way you engage in relationships today.

_____

_____

_____

Prompt 3: Identify a Prominent Event

Identify a prominent event from your childhood that caused pain or trauma. Describe the experience and explore how it continues to affect your current emotional triggers and your reactions to stress or conflict in your life.

_____

_____

_____

_____

_____

Prompt 4: Consider Your Early Interactions

Consider your early friendships and social interactions. Were there experiences of rejection or bullying that impacted you? Write about these moments and examine how they may influence feelings of inadequacy or fear in your adult relationships.

_____

_____

_____

Emotional Mapping Exercises

Activity: Create a Map

Create an emotional trigger map. This is how to start:

1) On a blank page, draw a large circle in the center and label it "Emotional Triggers."

2) From this central circle, branch out smaller circles for various emotional responses (e.g., anger, sadness, fear).

3) For each emotional response, connect lines to:

    a) specific childhood experiences or events that may have triggered these feelings.

    b) current situations where these emotional responses occur.

    c) people involved in these triggers (family, friends, colleagues).

4) Review your map for patterns. What childhood experiences appear linked to your emotional responses today? How can understanding these connections provide insights into your behavior?

_____

_____

_____

Reflective Activities

Activity 1: Trigger Exploration Worksheet

- ❏ Write a list of three recent situations where you felt strong emotional reactions. For each, answer the following:

    - What was the situation?

    - What emotions did you feel?

    - Can you trace these emotions back to a childhood experience? If yes, describe it.

    - How might recognizing these connections alter your approach to similar situations in the future?

_____

_____

_____

Activity 2: Patterns in Relationships Journal

- ❏ Reflect on your past and current relationships. Identify at least three recurring patterns (for example, fear of intimacy or attracting toxic partners).

- ❏ For each pattern, provide:

    - a description of the observed pattern.

    - how it may connect to unmet childhood needs or unresolved emotional triggers.

    - one action step you can take to break free from this pattern moving forward.

_____

_____

_____

Activity 3: Mind–Body Connection Reflection

- ❑ Contemplate how unresolved emotional triggers might be impacting you physically. Do you experience symptoms such as tension, headaches, or other physical manifestations during stressful moments?

- ❑ Write about these connections, including specific instances where physical symptoms coincide with emotional stress. How might addressing these emotional issues alleviate some of these physical symptoms?

_____

_____

_____

Looking Ahead

As you work through these exercises, notice how your understanding of emotional triggers evolves. In the next chapter, we'll explore the impact of early experiences on adult life.

Final Reflection

What's your key takeaway from this chapter?

_____

_____

What practice will you start with tomorrow?

_____

_____

Your Personal Notes

Use this space for additional thoughts and insights:

_____

_____

CHAPTER 3:

The Impact of Early Experiences on Adult Life

Do you struggle with self-esteem or emotional responses that seem rooted in your past? What patterns from your early life continue to shape your decisions today? You've learned how to identify triggers from early experiences shaping personal relationships, self-esteem, and emotional responses.

In this chapter, you will assess parental relationships and attachment styles, and explore some strategies to challenge your childhood patterns.

Quick Check-In Exercise

Before we explore your childhood patterns and their impact on your emotions, take a moment to check in with yourself:

Rate your current level (1–10):

Awareness of your childhood patterns: _____

How these patterns affect your relationships: _____

Comfort with exploring past experiences: _____

What emotions or thoughts are coming up as you begin this chapter?

_____

What specific patterns from your childhood do you want to address?

_____

_____

Parental Relationships and Attachment Styles

The way your caregivers responded to your needs shapes your expectations in relationships. For example:

- ❑ **Secure attachment:** If your needs were consistently met, you likely trust others and feel comfortable with intimacy

- ❑ **Anxious attachment:** If care was inconsistent, you might fear abandonment and seek reassurance

- ❑ **Avoidant attachment:** If emotional needs were dismissed, you might maintain distance in relationships

- ❑ **Disorganized attachment:** If care was erratic or frightening, you may experience confusion and fear in relationships, leading to unpredictable behaviors and difficulty in seeking comfort.

Quick Exercise

Think of a recent relationship conflict. How might your attachment style have influenced your reaction?

_____

_____

Interactive Exercise

Recall one of your earliest memories related to seeking comfort from a caregiver. Visualize the scene in detail. How did your caregiver respond to your needs in that moment? How did their response make you feel? Reflect on how that interaction may have shaped your attachment style and expectations in relationships.

_____

_____

_____

_____

Building Trust With Your Inner Child

Exercise 1: Making Promises

Write three promises to your inner child:

_____

_____

_____

Strategies to Challenge Your Childhood Patterns

In a world where nostalgia often blurs the lines of reality, uncovering and challenging the patterns we formed in childhood can lead to personal transformation.

Challenging Negative Beliefs

Breaking free from entrenched patterns and beliefs requires a structured approach toward healing. One effective strategy is actively challenging negative beliefs with affirmative statements representing a desired view of yourself. Consistently practicing this rewiring of thought patterns, you can align your self-perception with your aspirations rather than your past limitations.

Seeking Support and Community

Engaging in therapy or seeking support groups can enhance the healing process. A safe therapeutic environment allows you to delve deeper into your past wounds, offering professional insights and strategies for rewriting your narratives. Support groups create a communal aspect of healing, reinforcing the understanding that you are not alone in your struggles. By understanding the patterns shaped by your childhood and actively working to reshape them, you can carve a path to emotional freedom and a more fulfilling life.

Recognizing Dysfunctional Behaviors

Understanding the impact of early experiences on adult life is vital, especially when it comes to recognizing how deeply rooted childhood influences dictate your behaviors and emotional patterns. Attachment styles are a significant factor in this development, which are shaped in infancy through interactions with caregivers. Research has shown that these attachment styles often carry into adulthood, influencing how you emotionally connect with others (Lee, 2023).

Conflict Resolution Strategies

Your early experiences with conflict resolution also shape your adult communication strategies. That imprint remains if we grew up in environments where conflicts were either avoided or confrontationally addressed. Adults raised in such conditions may resort to avoidance or aggression in their disagreements. This can manifest as withdrawing from discussions or engaging in unproductive, combative exchanges.

To address these behaviors effectively, you must learn practical conflict-resolution skills. Strategies like active listening, calmly expressing emotions, and seeking compromise can transform personal and professional relationships. By recognizing past influences, adults can consciously choose healthier communication methods that lead to more constructive and peaceful interactions (Finch et al., 2024).

Overcoming the Fear of Vulnerability

A fear of vulnerability often emerges from past traumas, such as neglect or emotional invalidation, creating barriers to authentic connections in adulthood. When faced with situations requiring emotional exposure, individuals might retreat, shielding themselves from perceived threats of rejection or judgment. While this self-protective mechanism is understandable, it can obstruct the development of meaningful relationships and stifle personal growth.

Confronting and addressing this fear involves engaging with and healing past wounds. Therapeutic approaches, including cognitive-behavioral therapy and inner child work, can be incredibly beneficial in helping you confront your fears and teaching you to embrace vulnerability. In doing so, relationships can deepen, promoting greater fulfillment and intimacy (Lee, 2023).

More Practical Exercises

Explore a variety of engaging exercises designed to heal and reconnect with your inner child throughout this workbook.

Identifying Your Core Patterns

Instructions

Take time to reflect on three significant patterns in your adult life that you suspect may originate from childhood experiences. For each pattern, complete the following sections:

Pattern 1:

_____

How this pattern shows up in my life today:

_____

Possible childhood origins:

_____

How this impacts my current decisions and relationships:

_____

One small step I can take to begin shifting this pattern:

_____

Pattern 2:

_____

How this pattern shows up in my life today:

_____

Possible childhood origins:

_____

How this impacts my current decisions and relationships:

_____

One small step I can take to begin shifting this pattern:

___

Pattern 3:

___

How this pattern shows up in my life today:

___

Possible childhood origins:

___

How this impacts my current decisions and relationships:

___

One small step I can take to begin shifting this pattern:

___

Recognizing Unhealthy Relationship Patterns

To break free from relationship patterns rooted in childhood, try this exercise:

1) List your last three significant relationships.

2) Identify common themes or dynamics.

3) Reflect on how these mirror your childhood relationships.

4) Write down alternative responses that would better serve your adult needs.

___

Journaling Prompts

Prompt 1: A Turning Point

Reflect on a significant turning point in your life that you believe was influenced by your childhood experiences. Describe this event in detail, including your thoughts and feelings. How do you think your early experiences shaped your reaction to this event?

Prompt 2: Adult Relationship Patterns

Identify a recurring theme in adult relationships (like attracting similar partners or struggling with commitment). Write about how these patterns might relate to your childhood experiences. What core messages about relationships did you learn as a child that may be influencing your current behaviors?

Prompt 3: Moments of Self-Sabotage

Consider moments when you've engaged in self-sabotage (like procrastination and avoidance of opportunities). Journal about early experiences that may have instilled your fear of success or failure. How do these moments of self-sabotage reflect your inner beliefs from childhood?

Emotional Mapping Exercises

Activity: Create a Life Pattern Map

1) At the center of a blank page, write "Adult Patterns" and draw a circle around it.

2) Branch out into smaller circles for different behaviors or relationship patterns you recognize (like fear of intimacy and conflict avoidance).

3) For each pattern, draw lines connecting them to childhood experiences that may have shaped these behaviors (like family dynamics and caregiver relationships).

4) Reflect on your map. What connections can you make? How are these patterns reinforcing one another in your current life?

MY LIFE PATTERN MAP

Reflective Activities

Activity 1: Behavioral Reflection Worksheet

- ❏ Select a dysfunctional behavior you wish to change (e.g., avoidance, aggression during conflicts). Write about specific instances when you exhibited this behavior.

- ❏ Explore how your childhood experiences may have influenced this behavior for each instance. What messages did you learn that may have led to this reaction?

- ❏ Reflect on how you would like to respond differently in similar situations. What supportive phrases or strategies can you adopt to facilitate this change?

_____

_____

_____

Activity 2: Attachment Style Reflection

- ❏ Briefly research the different attachment styles (secure, anxious, avoidant, disorganized). Based on your relationships and interactions, identify your attachment style.

- ❏ Write about how your childhood experiences contributed to this attachment style. What were the relationships like with your caregivers?

- ❏ Consider how this awareness can lead you to make more intentional choices in future relationships. What new habits can you cultivate for healthier connections?

_____

_____

_____

Activity 3: Role Model Evaluation

- ❏ Reflect on the influential figures in your childhood (parents, guardians, mentors). List the behaviors or traits you admired in them and write about how these influences shaped your behaviors.

- ❏ Evaluate whether these learned behaviors have been helpful or harmful in your adult life. Which ones would you like to keep, and which would you prefer to change?

- ❏ Based on this reflection, set a goal to adopt healthier behaviors as you navigate future relationships and interactions.

_____

_____

_____

Looking Ahead

As you work through these exercises, consider how your early experiences may continue to shape your self-esteem and emotional responses today. In the next chapter, we will delve deeper into the impact of specific emotional triggers and explore strategies for cultivating emotional balance in your life.

Final Reflection

What's your key takeaway from this chapter?

_____

_____

What practice will you start with tomorrow?

_____

_____

Your Personal Notes

Use this space for additional thoughts and insights:

_____

_____

_____

CHAPTER 4:

Awareness and Recognition in Healing

Are you feeling disconnected from your emotional responses in daily life? Do you wish to explore the roots of your feelings and how they manifest in your behavior? Opening up to the idea of self-awareness can lead to great discoveries about yourself. This chapter encourages you to embark on an exploratory journey, inviting you to engage with your emotional landscape in new and meaningful ways.

Quick Check-In Exercise

Before we explore your emotional responses and self-awareness, take a moment to check in with yourself:

Rate your current level (1–10):

Awareness of your emotional responses: _____

Understanding of your triggers: _____

Comfort with exploring your emotions: _____

What emotions or thoughts are surfacing as you begin this chapter?

_____

What specific areas of your emotional landscape do you wish to explore?

_____

_____

Developing Self-Awareness of Emotional Responses

Beginning the journey of self-awareness regarding our emotional responses is a transformative experience that can lead to healing and personal growth. By understanding the triggers that evoke our emotional reactions, we empower ourselves to connect these feelings to past experiences and explore their origins.

Doing a Situation Analysis

The first step in exploring emotional triggers is recognizing how specific situations or stimuli can spark strong responses. Whether it's a particular place, sound, or phrase, these triggers often unveil unresolved issues from our past (Godreau, 2024). For example, an unexpected comment during a meeting might suddenly trigger feelings of anxiety reminiscent of similar criticisms faced in childhood. Acknowledging these connections creates an opportunity for deeper investigation into why these emotions arise, ultimately offering a more straightforward path forward.

Interactive Exercise: Emotion Connection

Connect your current emotions to past experiences to enhance self-awareness.

Instructions

- ❑ **Choose an emotion:** Select an emotion you've recently experienced. Write it at the center of a page.
- ❑ **Identify triggers:** Reflect on the event that triggered this emotion. What happened? Who was involved?
- ❑ **Connect to the past:** Think of any past experiences that evoke a similar feeling. Write down these memories and their connections to your current emotion.
- ❑ **Identify patterns:** What themes do you notice between your past experiences and current responses? How have these shaped your reactions today?
- ❑ **Action step:** Write down one actionable step you can take to address this emotion in the future, such as practicing mindfulness or reframing your thoughts.

_____

_____

Mindfulness as a Framework

Mindfulness is a powerful tool for enhancing emotional awareness. It allows us to observe our emotions as they unfold without judgment. This nonjudgmental approach creates a safe space to understand and accept our feelings rather than push them away. Mindfulness techniques—such as grounding exercises or short meditations—allow us to anchor ourselves in the present moment, which can significantly reduce the immediate emotional surge triggered by various stimuli (Lee-Hawkins, 2024).

Exercise: Inner Child Self-Hug

To create a deeper connection with your inner child, practice the inner child self-hug. Find a quiet space and sit comfortably. With your arms wrapped around your body, visualize hugging your younger self, allowing warmth and love to embrace you. As you breathe deeply, acknowledge their feelings of vulnerability, and offer reassurance that they are safe now. Jot down any notes from the experience below.

_____

_____

_____

Strategies for Self-Observation

Developing self-awareness involves employing effective strategies for self-observation. Start by paying attention to your daily interactions and noting when recurring emotional themes arise. Journaling can be particularly useful in tracking moments when heightened emotions occur but also consider incorporating audio reflections or body-based practices to deepen your awareness of bodily sensations in response to emotions.

Seeking Feedback to Uncover Blind Spots

Another valuable step in enhancing emotional awareness is seeking feedback from trusted friends or therapists. Others may recognize patterns in our behavior that we're often too close to see, or they may offer compassionate insights that illuminate our emotional responses. Sharing your experiences with someone who can guide you through self-reflection deepens your understanding of yourself and expands the scope of your self-awareness.

Incorporating Mindfulness Into Your Day

Make mindfulness a part of your daily life. Set aside specific moments for mindfulness practices, such as breathing exercises or simply observing your surroundings. Regularly tune into your emotional landscape to build an understanding and patience for yourself.

Establishing a Journaling Routine

Structure conscious self-observation through a dedicated journaling practice. Set a specific time, perhaps at the end of the day, to reflect on events and emotional reactions that stood out to you. Consider questions like: "What triggered my response?" and "How did I feel afterward?" Integrating this reflection into your routine helps cultivate consistent insight into your emotional patterns, enabling you to understand your responses better.

More Practical Exercises

Explore a variety of engaging exercises designed to reconnect with and nurture your inner child throughout this workbook.

Journaling Prompts

Prompt 1: Surprised by Emotion

Think of a moment in the past week when a particular emotion surprised you (e.g., unexpected anger or overwhelming sadness). Describe what happened leading up to that emotional reaction and your immediate thoughts. What deeper feelings or unresolved issues does this reaction seem to reflect?

_____

_____

Prompt 2: Strong Reactions

Reflect on a time you reacted strongly to a minor situation. What was the trigger, and how did it make you feel? Explore how this reaction could be signaling a past emotional wound. What insights can you draw from this experience about your triggers? How can you prepare for similar situations in the future?

_____

Prompt 3: Shift in Emotional State

Identify three recent scenarios where you noticed a shift in your emotional state. For each document, write down:

- ❏ the situation that triggered the change
- ❏ The emotional response you experienced
- ❏ any patterns or themes you observe in these triggers

Reflect on how recognizing these patterns might help you respond differently moving forward.

_____

_____

Mapping Emotional Awareness

Activity: Create an Emotional Awareness Map

1) Draw a large circle in the center of a blank page labeled "Emotional Awareness."

2) Branch out into smaller circles for different emotions you've experienced recently (e.g., frustration, joy, fear).

3) For each emotion, explore:

    a) What specific situations or people trigger these emotions?

    b) How these emotions affect your thoughts, actions, and decisions.

    c) Any links to past experiences that shape your current responses.

4) Reflect on your map. What new insights about yourself and your emotional landscape can you identify? How might this awareness guide your responses in the future?

_____

_____

EMOTIONAL AWARENESS MAP

Reflective Activities

Activity 1: Emotional Climate Journal

- ❑ Over the next week, keep an "Emotional Climate Journal" where you note your emotional state at various points throughout the day. Include context, thoughts, and physical sensations tied to these emotions.

- ❑ Review your entries at the end of the week and highlight any recurring emotions or themes. What do these insights reveal about your emotional patterns? How can you use this awareness to foster healthier emotional responses?

_____

_____

Activity 2: Explore Alternative Emotional Responses

- ❑ Choose one consistent emotional trigger from your reflections. Instead of your typical response, brainstorm three alternative reactions that you can practice in the face of this trigger.

- ❑ Write a plan detailing how to implement these new responses when the trigger occurs. Include strategies for grounding yourself or centering your emotions before reacting.

- ❑ After trying it out, write a journal about the experience: How did employing a new response make you feel? What did you learn about yourself and your emotions through this process?

_____

_____

Activity 3: Guided Audio Exercise

Consider listening to a guided audio meditation focused on self-exploration. This can facilitate a connection with your deeper emotions, providing a space to explore feelings related to past experiences. Write about your feelings.

_____

_____

Looking Ahead

As you engage with these exercises, reflect on how your emotional awareness impacts your interactions and personal growth. In the next chapter, we will explore the importance of recognizing the need for inner child healing and the steps you can take toward nurturing that aspect of yourself.

Final Reflection

What's your key takeaway from this chapter?

_____

_____

_____

_____

What practice will you start with tomorrow?

_____

_____

_____

_____

Your Personal Notes

Use this space for additional thoughts and insights:

_____

_____

_____

_____

_____

_____

CHAPTER 5:

Recognizing the Need for Inner Child Healing

Are you aware of the value of inner child healing in your life, and do you find yourself reflecting on the experiences that have shaped your emotional well-being? Have you considered the techniques that can help you identify when such healing is necessary, and are you ready to nurture the often-overlooked aspects of your youthful self?

This chapter explores methods to connect with your inner child, including journaling, writing letters to your younger self, and creating gratitude lists for personal growth. Are you brave enough to embrace a happier life? Let's start!

Quick Check-In Exercise

Before we explore recognizing your need for inner child healing, take a moment to check in with yourself:

Rate your current level (1–10):

❑ Awareness of your inner child's needs: _____

❑ Readiness to explore healing: _____

❑ Current self-care practice: _____

What brings you to this chapter today?

_____

What aspects of healing feel most urgent?

_____

Why Journaling Is Important for Inner Child Healing

Journaling is a life-changing tool for self-exploration, providing a powerful pathway to understanding your inner child's needs. As an adult, it's easy to overlook the joys of childhood, but reflecting on those moments can be an incredibly healing practice. When you revisit the simple pleasures of youth—like playing outside, spending time with family, or engaging in creative activities—you can reconnect with the sources of happiness and emotional fulfillment that shaped who you are today.

Exploring Childhood Fears Through Writing

Many of us carry childhood fears into adulthood without fully realizing their ongoing impact. Journaling about these fears allows you to explore their origins and recognize how they affect your current feelings and challenges. Whether it's a fear of the dark, being alone, or not measuring up academically, identifying these childhood anxieties can offer valuable insights into your adult life. Examine how these fears manifest today, to gain clarity on your emotional hurdles, creating a pathway for effectively addressing them.

Writing Letters to Your Inner Child

One particularly helpful journaling exercise involves writing letters to your inner child. This practice allows you to engage in a compassionate dialogue with the parts of yourself that may have been neglected or hurt. Expressing understanding and forgiveness through this process, you can begin to address past wounds with empathy. These letters serve as nurturing gestures, assuring your inner child that their feelings are valid and deserving of care. This act helps heal old hurts and encourages a caring relationship with yourself, promoting ongoing emotional well-being.

Creating a Gratitude List for Childhood Joys

In addition to addressing fears and healing wounds, crafting a gratitude list centered on positive childhood experiences can significantly contribute to your growth and healing. By listing events or relationships that brought joy or a sense of security during your formative years, you shift your focus to nurturing and fulfilling aspects of your life. Recognizing these moments bolsters your sense of identity and resilience, reminding you of the support systems and positive influences that shaped your development.

The Therapeutic Function of Reflecting on Joy

Reflecting on joyful childhood experiences isn't just an exercise in nostalgia; it carries essential therapeutic value. Immersing yourself in memories of joy creates a counterbalance to the struggles you face today. This practice allows you to reclaim parts of your identity that may have been overshadowed by adult responsibilities or traumas, rejuvenating your spirit and providing hope as you navigate current challenges.

Understanding the Impact of Childhood Experiences

Exploring childhood fears through journaling also paves the way for self-discovery. It encourages you to consider how these early experiences shaped your worldview and emotional landscape. The fears you faced back then may still trigger responses in your adult life. Recognizing these patterns empowers you to break free from them. This process helps you develop healthier coping mechanisms and boosts your emotional resilience, enhancing your capacity for self-compassion and growth.

Redefining Your Relationship With the Past

The act of writing letters to your inner child offers an introspective avenue to connect with your past self. It provides a safe space to articulate emotions that were perhaps unexpressed or misunderstood at the time. This journey allows you to redefine your relationship with the past, transforming it into a source of wisdom rather than pain. Addressing your inner child with kindness and acceptance lays the groundwork for a healthier, more integrated sense of self.

Acknowledging Your Growth Through Gratitude

Crafting a gratitude list that highlights childhood experiences enables you to honor the foundational aspects of your upbringing. This practice helps cultivate a mindset recognizing personal growth as a journey enriched by trials and triumphs. When you can see the full spectrum of your experiences, your personal narrative becomes more balanced and affirming, reminding you of your strengths and the supportive elements still influencing who you are today.

Bridging the Gap Between Past and Present

Encouraging self-exploration through journaling is not just about recounting the past; it's a dynamic process that bridges the gap between who you were and who you are becoming. Engaging in reflective writing helps you develop a deeper connection with your inner child, acknowledging their presence and importance in your life. This journey of self-discovery is vital for healing and nurturing your emotional self.

Interactive Exercise: Healing Readiness Assessment

Take a moment to reflect on your current state of healing:

_____

_____

What signals is your inner child sending?

- ❑ Emotional signals: _____
- ❑ Physical signals: _____
- ❑ Relationship patterns: _____
- ❑ Recurring thoughts: _____

Rate your readiness to address each area (1–10):

- ❑ Emotional healing: _____
- ❑ Past trauma work: _____
- ❑ Relationship healing _____
- ❑ Self-trust building: _____

What support do you need to begin?

_____

Steps to Create a Personal Healing Plan

Creating a personal healing plan for inner child work is a deeply life-changing process that starts with understanding your unique emotional needs and experiences. Your childhood leaves a distinct imprint that continues to influence your adult life. You can gain clarity and direction by identifying your healing priorities, laying the foundation for manageable approaches that promote progress and well-being.

Step 1: Identify Priorities for Healing

Recognizing your healing priorities is essential for providing clarity in your journey. This allows you to focus on specific aspects of your emotional landscape that need attention. Reflecting on past experiences can shed light on areas where unmet childhood needs may still impact your life today. Ask yourself: What recurring themes or feelings arise when you think about your childhood? Which memories trigger powerful emotions?

Acknowledging these elements can help you create a targeted approach. For instance, if feelings of abandonment surface as a significant wound, recognizing its influence on your current relationships or self-esteem can direct your healing efforts. Focusing on what feels most pressing or triggering streamlines the healing process, ensuring you address the issues that are ready for healing.

Step 2: Set Realistic Goals

Setting realistic goals is important for sustaining motivation throughout your transformative journey. Establishing specific, measurable, and achievable targets fosters progress while instilling a sense of accomplishment. Begin by defining what healing success means to you—whether it's developing healthier relationships, finding inner peace, or building resilience against emotional distress.

Break larger aspirations into smaller, manageable steps. For example, if your goal is to enhance self-compassion, commit to daily affirmations or incorporate journaling practices that promote positive self-talk. Setting milestones provides tangible evidence of your growth, celebrating small victories fuels persistence, and acknowledging that healing is an ongoing process keeps your expectations grounded.

Step 3: Develop Coping Strategies

Developing coping strategies enhances your self-efficacy, equipping you with effective methods to manage emotional triggers. These tools serve as anchors during overwhelming moments, offering stability amid turbulent emotions. Incorporating techniques like meditation, mindfulness, and breathing exercises can ground you in the present, reduce anxiety, and foster inner calm.

Consider exploring creative outlets, such as art or music therapy, to express emotions nonverbally. Journaling is another powerful tool that allows for introspection and reflection on emotional patterns. Engaging in physical activities, like yoga or walking, further supports emotional regulation by promoting the mind–body connection and releasing built-up tension.

Experiment with different coping strategies to discover what resonates with you and tailor your toolkit to suit your needs. Flexibility is key; as you evolve, your preferred methods may change. Regularly reassess and adapt your strategies to ensure they remain effective in navigating life's challenges.

Step 4: Establish a Support System

Building a robust support system is vital for creating an encouraging network that reduces feelings of isolation during the healing process. Sharing your experiences with trusted friends, family, or support groups can alleviate loneliness and provide comfort through shared understanding. Reach out to mental health professionals specializing in inner child work for guidance, validation, and expert insights.

Therapists experienced in early-life modalities can facilitate deeper exploration, unearthing buried emotions and fostering healing. Participate in communities focused on inner child healing, whether locally or online, where empathetic listening and mutual encouragement thrive.

A strong support system can encompass various forms of assistance, from emotional support to practical help. Identify key individuals who can fulfill different roles—a friend to confide in, a mentor for advice, or a therapist offering professional guidance. Diverse connections enhance resilience and cushion your healing journey's inevitable ups and downs.

Embracing Your Personal Healing Journey

Developing a personalized approach to inner child healing empowers you to reclaim control over your narrative. By identifying your healing priorities, setting realistic goals, developing effective coping strategies, and establishing supportive networks, you lay the groundwork for meaningful transformation. Though challenging, this journey can lead to self-discovery and renewed emotional freedom, with each step bringing you closer to a more harmonious self.

More Practical Exercises

Explore a variety of engaging exercises designed to reconnect with and nurture your inner child throughout this workbook.

Journaling Prompts

Prompt 1: Happies Childhood Memories

Take a moment to write about your three happiest childhood memories. What made these moments special, and how did they impact your sense of self? Consider how revisiting these joyful experiences can illuminate what brings you fulfillment today. How can you intentionally create similar joyful experiences in your adult life, and what steps will you take to incorporate them?

_____

_____

_____

Prompt 2: Childhood Fears List

Create a list of the childhood fears that still resonate in your life today. Describe how these fears impact your thoughts, actions, or relationships. Reflect on specific situations where these fears have manifested—how have they held you back? What empowering steps can you take to confront and transform these fears into sources of strength?

_____

_____

_____

Prompt 3: Gratitude List

Compose a gratitude list highlighting positive aspects or memories from your childhood, even amid the difficulties. Reflect on how these experiences contributed to your growth. Consider how you can celebrate these aspects moving forward—what practices can you implement to honor and integrate this gratitude into your present life?

_____

_____

_____

_____

_____

Emotional Mapping Exercises

Activity: Create an Inner Child Emotional Map for Healing

1) **Title your map:** In the center of a blank page, write "Inner Child Emotional Pattern Healing" and encircle it.

2) **Branch out emotions:** From this central circle, create smaller circles for different emotions you associate with your childhood (such as joy, fear, disappointment, sadness, or longing).

3) **Explore each emotion:**

    a) For each emotion, reflect on specific childhood experiences that evoke these feelings. Note how these experiences have shaped your current adult emotional responses and behaviors.

    b) Ask yourself guiding questions:

        i. What was happening during these significant moments?

        ii. How did these emotions manifest in your childhood, and how do they continue to influence your adult life?

        iii. What needs were unmet in those moments?

4) **Focus on healing:** After you've completed your map, take time to analyze the emotional patterns:

    a) Which emotions stand out as most significant in your life?

    b) How do these emotions influence your thoughts, decisions, and relationships today?

    c) Identify one specific emotional area that deeply resonates with you and that you'd like to focus on healing.

5) **Action steps for healing:** For the emotion you've chosen to nurture, write down tangible steps you can take to address and heal this area. Consider:

    a) What self-compassion practices could help you process this emotion?

    b) Can specific activities or rituals facilitate healing (like mindfulness, creative expression, or speaking to your inner child through journaling)?

    c) How can you integrate positive affirmations or supportive dialogues to comfort and reassure your inner child moving forward?

_____

_____

INNER CHILD EMOTIONAL MAP FOR HEALING

Reflective Activities

Activity 1: Define Your Healing Priorities

- ❑ Write down three key areas of your emotional life that require immediate focus. Reflect on why these areas are significant to you. What specific feelings or behaviors are you experiencing related to these priorities?

- ❑ Choose one priority to concentrate on and brainstorm actionable steps to nurture healing in this area over the next month. What resources or practices can support you in this journey?

_____

_____

Activity 2: Goal Setting for Healing Your Inner Child

- ❑ Formulate three specific, measurable, and achievable goals tailored to your inner child healing journey. For instance, set a goal like: "I will dedicate 30 minutes each week to engaging in a creative activity that my inner child would enjoy."

- ❑ Reflect on why each goal holds importance for you and detail how you will measure your progress. Consider what support or accountability you may need to achieve these goals.

_____

_____

Activity 3: Develop Personalized Coping Strategies

- ❑ Compile a list of five coping strategies that resonate with you for managing emotional triggers linked to your inner child. Include strategies like deep breathing, grounding techniques, creative expression (art, music), or mindfulness practices.

- ❑ For each strategy, identify a specific situation where you can practice it in the upcoming week. How will you remind yourself to use these strategies when those emotional triggers arise?

_____

_____

Looking Ahead

As you work through these exercises, notice how your understanding of your healing needs evolves. In the next workbook, we'll explore inner child reparenting techniques.

Final Reflection

What's your key takeaway from this chapter?

_____

_____

_____

_____

What practice will you start with tomorrow?

_____

_____

_____

_____

Your Personal Notes

Use this space for additional thoughts and insights:

_____

_____

_____

_____

_____

CONCLUSION

By now you know that understanding your inner child is key to healing emotionally—it affects how you see yourself and respond to feelings. Recognizing your inner child helps you learn to accept and be kind to yourself, allowing you to change the way you think about your self-worth. Looking into emotional triggers connected to childhood experiences allows you to see patterns in how you behave as an adult, which can help you manage your emotions better. By identifying these triggers, you understand that past experiences can influence your reactions without you realizing it, which makes it possible for you to respond to your emotions more intentionally.

Improving self-awareness about your emotional responses helps you notice and understand your emotional patterns, leading to better control over your feelings and healing. Paying attention to how strong your emotions are, especially from small triggers, can reveal unresolved issues and show you a way to heal and understand yourself better. Creating a personalized approach to healing your inner child ensures that you engage in helpful practices that meet your unique emotional needs. Building a support system and setting realistic goals make the healing process a shared journey, encouraging accountability and growth together. If you follow these steps, you will start a journey toward inner peace and emotional freedom.

If you've enjoyed this workbook, join us again in Workbook 2: Inner Child Reparenting: Practical Tools to Build Emotional Strength, Set Boundaries, and Foster Self-Compassion to continue your personal development journey.

BOOK 2

Inner Child Reparenting

Practical Tools to Build Emotional Strength, Set Boundaries, and Foster Self-Compassion

INTRODUCTION

Have you ever felt a wave of emotions that confused you about its origins? Certain sights, sounds, or situations can evoke responses that seem disproportionate to the present moment. If this resonates with you, you're not alone. We are influenced by unseen forces shaped by past experiences that continue to impact our daily lives. Understanding how your history shapes your present is the first step toward healing and achieving a more balanced life.

Welcome to *Inner Child Reparenting: Practical Tools to Build Emotional Strength, Set Boundaries, and Foster Self-Compassion*. This workbook invites you to reconnect with a part of yourself that holds influence: your inner child. Think of yourself as youthful, innocent, and sometimes hurt. Inner child work is about nurturing this aspect of yourself, allowing for the healing of wounds that may unconsciously guide your current behaviors and feelings. This journey is a life-changing process enabling your adult self to provide the love, support, and guidance lacking in your earlier years.

Why start this journey now? Reparenting your inner child is essential for emotional resilience and personal growth. It involves forming a positive relationship with your inner child by recognizing and addressing unmet needs from your past. Engaging in this process creates a solid foundation for developing healthier emotional responses and forging deeper, more meaningful relationships.

Throughout this guide, you'll encounter practical tools to facilitate self-discovery and healing. These include guided visualizations that help you create safe mental spaces for healing, mindfulness exercises that promote present-moment awareness, and journaling prompts that encourage reflection on behaviors tied to unmet needs.

Establishing healthy boundaries is another aspect of personal growth, often rooted in childhood experiences. Setting limits reinforces your sense of autonomy and facilitates balanced interactions. Learning self-soothing techniques empowers you to handle emotional triggers effectively, promoting resilience in the face of challenges.

As you explore these tools, remember that this journey is not about fixing what's broken—because you are not. It's about honoring all parts of yourself and discovering the fullness of your being. Each exercise is a gateway to strengthen your understanding, paving the way toward emotional well-being and self-compassion.

The key chapters systematically guide you through the process of healing:

- ❏ **The Basics of Reparenting Your Inner Child**
- ❏ **Developing Emotional Resilience and Self-Love**
- ❏ **Setting and Maintaining Healthy Boundaries**
- ❏ **Practicing Self-Soothing Techniques**
- ❏ **Creating a Safe Emotional Environment**

This workbook is a supportive companion as you seek personal growth, improved relationships, or professional development. Approach this journey with compassion and patience as you uncover the roots of your present emotions. Each chapter will give you insightful tools for cultivating a healthier, more loving relationship with yourself.

Let your curiosity guide you as you begin this life-changing journey. Your inner child awaits, ready to walk alongside you toward a future filled with possibilities and healing.

CHAPTER 1:

The Basics of Reparenting Your Inner Child

Reparenting your inner child is a journey that helps you connect with a vital part of yourself essential for personal growth and healing. This chapter invites you to explore practical ways to nurture your inner child, addressing past wounds and unmet needs that impact your life today.

This chapter discusses caring practices that allow you to give yourself love and support that makes reparenting your inner child possible.

Quick Check-In Exercise

Before we explore reparenting your inner child, take a moment to check in with yourself:

Rate your current level (1–10):

- ❑ Understanding of reparenting: _____
- ❑ Connection with your inner child: _____
- ❑ Readiness to nurture yourself: _____

What kind of parent would you like to be to your inner child?

_____

_____

What support do you wish you had received as a child?

_____

_____

Interactive Reflection: Write a Letter to Your Inner Child

Take a moment to reflect on your relationship with your inner child. Write a letter to them, explaining how you will take care of them now. Share your commitments to providing love, support, and understanding. This exercise sets the tone for your journey ahead.

_____

_____

_____

Understanding Reparenting

Reparenting is about nurturing the inner child previously neglected or wounded during childhood. It offers an opportunity to address emotional needs, develop self-esteem, and establish healthier emotional patterns. Instead of dwelling on abstract concepts, we will dive into actionable steps you can take to support your healing.

Activities such as drawing, writing, or playing can help you reconnect with the joyful aspects of childhood. By embracing these creative outlets, you can nurture your inner child's needs and enhance emotional regulation.

Practicing mindfulness is an essential tool in reparenting. Being present allows you to observe your emotional responses without judgment. This chapter incorporates mindfulness strategies to facilitate awareness of triggers and patterns stemming from childhood experiences that influence your current emotional landscape.

More Practical Exercises

These exercises will guide you in nurturing your inner child while enhancing your self-awareness and promoting emotional healing.

Journaling Prompts

Prompt 1: Spending Time With Your Inner Child

Picture a day you could spend with your inner child. Write about the activities you would plan, such as playing games, reading stories, or going on adventures. Write below, describe your emotions toward your inner child and how these activities might help heal any past wounds.

___

___

Prompt 2: Visualize Your Inner Child's Favorite Place

Visualize your inner child's favorite place, whether real or imaginary. Write a detailed journal entry describing this space, focusing on its sights, sounds, and smells. What feelings does this environment evoke in your inner child? Explore how you can incorporate aspects of this safe space into your everyday life, creating a sense of comfort and belonging.

___

___

Prompt 3: Inner Child Song-Finder

Think of five songs that would resonate with your inner child and jot them down in your journal. For each song, write about the emotions and memories it evokes. Reflect on how these songs connect to your inner child's feelings and dreams. Describe how developing a listening ritual around these songs can serve as a nurturing practice for your inner child.

___

___

Reflective Activities

Activity 1: Creating a Time Capsule

Think about creating a time capsule for your inner child. List five items you would include that represent both your childhood joys and the challenges you faced. After listing the items, reflect on how each one connects to your current emotional responses or behaviors. What does each item teach you about the needs of your inner child?

___

___

___

Activity 2: The What-If Game

Play the "What-If" game with your inner child's challenges. Write down a current challenge you are facing and consider how your inner child might have approached the same challenge years ago. List three different responses your inner child might have taken. Reflect on how these alternative approaches could inform your current strategy for dealing with this challenge.

_____

_____

Activity 3: Affirmation Art Project

On a piece of paper, create a piece of art that incorporates affirmations for your inner child. Use colors, shapes, and symbols that resonate with you. While creating this project, write down the affirmations you're including and explain why each affirmation is important. Reflect on how these affirmations can serve as a daily reminder of the love and support you can provide your inner child.

_____

_____

Looking Ahead

As you work through these exercises, notice how your relationship with your inner child evolves through reparenting. In the next chapter, we'll explore developing emotional resilience and self-love.

Final Reflection

What's your key takeaway from this chapter?

_____

_____

What practice will you start with tomorrow?

_____

_____

Your Personal Notes

Use this space for additional thoughts and insights:

CHAPTER 2:

Developing Emotional Resilience and Self-Love

Developing emotional resilience and self-love involves connecting deeply with your inner child—the part of you that holds the keys to past experiences shaping your current behaviors. This chapter offers practical techniques to strengthen this connection, providing tools for emotional healing and transformation.

The power of affirmations and mirror work unveils the potential of positive self-talk and reflective practices in fostering self-love and personal growth.

Quick Check-In Exercise

Before we explore emotional resilience and self-love, take a moment to check in with yourself:

Rate your current level (1–10):

- ❏ Emotional resilience: _____
- ❏ Self-love practice: _____
- ❏ Comfort with mirror work: _____

What makes you feel emotionally strong?

_____

How do you currently show yourself love?

_____

What aspect of self-love feels most challenging?

_____

Creating Your Personal Affirmations

Affirmations are positive statements that help rewrite negative self-narratives developed during childhood. When crafted with intention and practiced consistently, they can transform how you speak to yourself and reconnect you with your inner child.

Step 1: Identify Areas for Healing

Consider aspects of your life where you feel vulnerable or wounded. What messages did you need to hear as a child but didn't? What do you struggle to believe about yourself now?

Step 2: Craft Positive, Present-Tense Statements

Transform each need into an affirmation using "I am," "I deserve," or "I choose" statements. Make them specific, meaningful, and emotionally resonant.

Examples:

- ❑ "I am worthy of love exactly as I am."
- ❑ "I deserve to take up space and express my needs."
- ❑ "I choose to treat myself with the same kindness I offer others."
- ❑ "I am safe to feel all my emotions."
- ❑ "I trust my inner wisdom."

Step 3: Make Them Personal

Add details that make these affirmations uniquely yours. List specific qualities you value in yourself or particular situations where you need support.

Write Down Your Affirmations

_____

_____

Mirror Work Practice

Mirror work is a powerful technique that combines affirmations with direct eye contact in a mirror, creating a deeper connection with yourself.

Basic Mirror Work Practice

1) **Set up:** Find a private space with a mirror where you won't be disturbed. Keep your affirmations nearby.

2) **Center yourself:** Take three deep breaths, looking at yourself in the mirror.

3) **Make contact:** Look directly into your own eyes with soft focus. This may feel uncomfortable at first, but this discomfort is normal and will ease with practice.

4) **Speak with intention:** Say your chosen affirmation aloud while maintaining eye contact. Speak slowly and with conviction.

5) **Feel the emotion:** Allow yourself to experience whatever emotions arise—resistance, sadness, hope, or love.

6) **Close the practice:** Thank yourself for showing up, perhaps placing a hand on your heart in a gesture of self-compassion.

Progression of Mirror Work

- **Beginning (Week 1):** Start with 2–3 minutes daily using one simple affirmation like "I am worthy of love."

- **Intermediate (Weeks 2–3):** Extend to 5 minutes, adding affirmations specific to current challenges.

- **Advanced (Week 4+):** Practice for 5–10 minutes, adding spontaneous loving messages to yourself beyond prepared affirmations.

Implementing Your Affirmation Practice

- Choose optimal times: Morning (to set intention for the day) and evening (to reinforce positive self-messaging) work best for most people.

- Create environmental triggers: Place affirmation cards near your mirror, on your desk, or as phone reminders.

- ❏ Pair with other practices: Incorporate affirmations into journaling, visualization, or mindful movement practices mentioned throughout this workbook.

- ❏ Track your progress: Notice how your relationship with affirmations changes over time—initial resistance often transforms into deeper self-acceptance.

Measuring Effectiveness

Keep a weekly log noting

- ❏ which affirmations feel most powerful
- ❏ how your inner dialogue is changing
- ❏ moments when you naturally redirect negative self-talk
- ❏ physical sensations that accompany your practice

Remember: The power of affirmations comes through consistency and emotional connection. With practice, these new self-messages will gradually replace old, limiting beliefs instilled in childhood.

Weekly Affirmation Practice Log

Week: _____

Most Powerful Affirmations This Week

List your top 3 affirmations and rate their impact (1–10):

Affirmation 1:

_____

Impact rating: _____

Why it resonated:

_____

Affirmation 2:

_____

Impact rating: _____

Why it resonated:

_____

Affirmation 3:

_____

Impact rating: _____

Why it resonated:

_____

Inner Dialogue Changes

Notice shifts in your self-talk throughout the week:

Monday:_____

    ❏ Morning mood:_____

    ❏ Self-talk pattern: _____

    ❏ Changes noticed:_____

Wednesday: _____

    ❏ Morning mood:_____

    ❏ Self-talk pattern: _____

    ❏ Changes noticed:_____

Friday: _____

    ❏ Morning mood:_____

    ❏ Self-talk pattern: _____

❑ Changes noticed:_____

Sunday: _____

    ❑ Morning mood:_____

    ❑ Self-talk pattern: _____

Negative Self-Talk Redirects

Record moments when you caught and redirected negative self-talk:

Situation	Negative thought	How you redirected it

Physical Sensations During Practice

Morning practice:

    ❑ Body tension level (1–10): _____

    ❑ Breathing (shallow/deep): _____

    ❑ Overall comfort level: _____

    ❑ Notable sensations: _____

Evening practice:

- ❏ Body tension level (1–10): _____
- ❏ Breathing (shallow/deep): _____
- ❏ Overall comfort level: _____
- ❏ Notable sensations: _____

Weekly Progress Notes

Biggest challenge: _____

Proudest moment: _____

Key insight: _____

Next week's focus: _____

Example Entries

Most Powerful Affirmation

- ❏ "I am safe to express my feelings freely"
- ❏ Impact Rating: 8
- ❏ Why it resonated: Helped me speak up in a difficult meeting at work

Inner Dialogue Change

- ❏ Wednesday Morning mood: Anxious about presentation
- ❏ Self-talk pattern: Caught myself saying "I can't do this"
- ❏ Changes noticed: Used affirmation "I am capable and prepared" instead

Negative Self-Talk Redirect

- ❏ Situation: Made a mistake on project

- ❏ Negative Thought: "I always mess things up"
- ❏ How You Redirected It: "I'm learning and growing from this experience"

Physical Sensations During Practice
- ❏ Morning Practice: Body tension level: 7
- ❏ Breathing: Shallow at first, deepened with practice
- ❏ Overall comfort level: Improving
- ❏ Notable sensations: Shoulders relaxed after 5 minutes

Inner Child Connection Techniques

Building on our foundation of affirmations and mirror work, here are additional techniques to strengthen your connection with your inner child:

Mindful Reflection

Take time each day to sit quietly and invite your inner child's presence. As emotions or memories surface, acknowledge them without judgment. Use affirmations from the previous section to reassure your inner child when difficult feelings arise.

When childhood memories trigger shame or fear, gently repeat your core affirmation while visualizing your younger self.

Journaling as a Tool

Create an ongoing dialogue with your inner child through writing. Begin each journaling session by writing an affirmation at the top of the page, then allow your thoughts to flow freely.

After journaling, take one powerful insight to your mirror practice, speaking directly to your reflection about what you've discovered.

Visualization Techniques

Create a mental safe space where you can meet and interact with your inner child. Incorporate the affirmations you've developed as loving messages you share during these visualizations.

Use your personalized affirmations as the foundation for what you say to your inner child during visualization.

Engaging in Playful Activities

Reconnect with activities that brought you joy as a child. Before beginning, look in the mirror and affirm: "I deserve to experience joy and playfulness."

Notice how engaging in play affects how you see yourself. Return to the mirror after playful activities and observe any shifts in your expression.

More Practical Exercises

Explore a variety of engaging exercises designed to reconnect with and nurture your inner child throughout this workbook.

Journaling Prompts

Engage in these journaling prompts to nurture your inner child.

Prompt 1: Reflecting on Childhood Emotions

Spend some quiet time reflecting on a specific childhood memory that brings up strong feelings. Write about this experience in your journal. What emotions come up as you think about it? How do these emotions relate to how you deal with similar situations now? Recognize your feelings and show kindness to your younger self in your writing.

_____

_____

_____

_____

_____

Prompt 2: Letter to Your Younger Self

Write a letter to your younger self. Share your love and support. What kind words would you want to say? Think about the difficulties your younger self faced and how you can help them now. Include positive statements that lift their spirits.

_____

_____

_____

_____

Prompt 3: Creating Your Safe Space

Picture a safe place where you can connect with your inner child. Describe what this space looks like, what it smells like, and how it feels. How can this safe space give comfort and reassurance to your inner child? Think about how you can bring some of these elements into your everyday life

_____

_____

_____

_____

Prompt 4: Identifying Moments of Play

Think about a time when you felt really happy and playful. Write about that moment in your journal. What were you doing? How did it feel to forget about your worries and responsibilities? Think of ways to add more fun moments to your life to keep your inner child alive.

_____

_____

_____

_____

Reflective Exercises

Engage in these reflective exercises incorporating mirror work as far as possible.

Exercise 1: Enhanced Visualization With Affirmations

Spend 10–15 minutes in a quiet place, close your eyes, and imagine your inner child in a safe and loving environment. See them happy and free. Talk gently to your inner child. What do they want to tell you? How can you help and protect them? After this, write about what you experienced and learned in a journal.

_____

_____

_____

Exercise 2: Creating Mirror-Specific Affirmations

Pick one or two parts of your life where you want to become stronger or learn to love yourself more. Create 3–5 positive affirmations specifically designed for mirror work. These should address these aspects of yourself that feel vulnerable when you make eye contact in the mirror.

_____

_____

_____

Exercise 3: Tracking Emotional Changes

Create a journal page to track your feelings over the next month as you use positive statements and connect with your inner child. Write down important events, changes in how you think, and any new feelings of self-love. Think about how these activities are affecting your daily life and emotional health.

_____

_____

_____

_____

Exercise 4: Engaging in Play

Make a list of five activities that spark joy and playfulness within you. Choose one of these activities to engage in within the next week. After you have done the activity, reflect on how it felt to embrace playfulness. Did you notice any shifts in your mood or perspective afterward? Journal your thoughts and feelings.

___

___

___

Looking Ahead

As you work through these exercises, notice how your capacity for emotional resilience and self-love evolves. In the next chapter, we'll explore setting and maintaining healthy boundaries to further protect and nurture your inner child.

Final Reflection

What's your key takeaway from this chapter?

___

___

___

What practice will you start with tomorrow?

___

___

___

Your Personal Notes

Use this space for additional thoughts and insights:

___

___

CHAPTER 3:

Setting and Maintaining Healthy Boundaries

Setting and maintaining healthy boundaries is necessary for personal and emotional well-being. Boundaries define where you end and others begin, guiding interactions and protecting mental health. Despite their importance, many struggle to establish them, often feeling guilty or overwhelmed. This chapter explores effective strategies for confidently creating and maintaining boundaries that respect your needs.

Quick Check-In Exercise

Before we explore boundary setting, take a moment to check in with yourself:

_____
_____

Rate your current level (1–10):

❑ Ability to set boundaries: _____

❑ Comfort saying "no": _____

❑ Understanding of your limits: _____

What situations challenge your boundaries most?

_____
_____

How do you feel when setting boundaries?

_____

_____

The Importance of Boundaries

Knowing your limits is essential for emotional health. Boundaries serve as protective barriers, ensuring balanced and respectful relationships while guarding against emotional exhaustion and burnout. Establishing clear boundaries enhances communication, reduces misunderstandings, and fosters healthier connections, ultimately supporting your self-worth and emotional resilience.

Key Types of Boundaries

1) **Personal boundaries:** Define your own space and ensure your choices are respected.

2) **Emotional boundaries:** Protect your feelings from manipulation or undue influence by others.

3) **Physical boundaries:** Determine how and when others can engage with your physical space.

Understanding these types allows for a tailored approach to boundary-setting, helping uphold your self-respect and establish fulfilling relationships.

Communicating Your Boundaries

To effectively set boundaries, articulate your needs clearly using specific strategies:

1) **"I" statements:** Use "I" statements to communicate feelings without blaming others. For example, "I feel unsupported when my ideas are interrupted" fosters constructive dialogue and reduces defensiveness.

2) **Active listening:** Demonstrate respect and empathy by listening attentively. Use nonverbal cues like nodding and making eye contact to show engagement. Reflect back what you hear to confirm understanding.

3) **Clear expectations**: Clearly outline your expectations in various settings to prevent misunderstandings. For instance, in a shared workspace, agree on expectations for communication and task responsibilities.

4) **Nonverbal cues:** Ensure your body language aligns with your verbal message. A confident posture and appropriate eye contact reinforce what you're saying.

5) **Offering alternatives:** When denying a request, suggest alternatives to show flexibility while maintaining your limits. For example, instead of saying, "No, I can't help," you might say, "I can't assist right now, but how about we find another time to discuss?"

6) **Staying composed:** Maintaining professionalism during boundary discussions is vital. Remain calm and respectful, focusing on addressing concerns constructively.

Real-Life Scripts for Boundary Setting

- ❑ **Saying no without guilt:** "I appreciate the offer, but I need to prioritize my time right now. Let's schedule another time to connect."

- ❑ **Expressing needs in relationships:** "I value our time together, but I need more personal space to recharge. Can we find a balance that works for both of us?"

- ❑ **Declining unwanted advice:** "I appreciate your concern, but I prefer to explore my options on my own right now. Thank you for understanding."

- ❑ **Requesting respect for personal time:** "I need some quiet time to focus on my work. I appreciate your understanding and support in keeping this time focused."

- ❑ **Setting limits on social media engagement:** "I enjoy reconnecting online, but I've decided to limit my social media use for my mental well-being. Let's catch up in person instead!"

Jot down if you've tried to use these scripts and what the outcomes were.

_____

_____

Interactive Exercise: Boundary Mapping

Take a moment to map out your current boundaries in different areas of life:

Personal Space Boundaries

- ❏ What feels comfortable: _____
- ❏ What feels uncomfortable: _____
- ❏ My ideal personal space looks like: _____

Time Boundaries

- ❏ Activities that drain my energy: _____
- ❏ Activities that energize me: _____
- ❏ My ideal schedule would include: _____

Emotional Boundaries

- ❏ Feelings I'm comfortable sharing: _____
- ❏ Feelings I prefer to keep private: _____
- ❏ My emotional limits are: _____

Relationship Boundaries

- ❏ What I need in relationships: _____
- ❏ What I won't accept: _____
- ❏ My non-negotiables are: _____

More Practical Exercises

Explore a variety of engaging exercises designed to reconnect with and nurture your inner child throughout this workbook.

Journaling Prompts

Prompt 1: Identifying Your Boundaries

Think about the limits you have in different parts of your life, like your relationships, work, and your feelings. Write about the boundaries you feel are strong and those that need more support. What situations show how important these boundaries are?

_____

_____

Prompt 2: Exploring Emotional Limits

Think about a time when someone upset you by not respecting your feelings. Describe what happened and how it made you feel. How could you have told them your limits better? What will you do differently next time?

_____

_____

Prompt 3: Crafting "I" Statements

Think of a time when you felt upset because someone didn't respect your limits or didn't communicate well. Write a statement that explains how you felt, what the other person did that bothered you, and what you need from them. How can sharing your needs help set clear limits in the future?

_____

_____

Prompt 4: Visualizing Your Boundaries

Imagine a situation where you clearly explain your limits. In your journal, write about this scene—who is there, what you say, and how others react. Think about how this visualization makes you feel and how it might affect your real-life interactions.

_____

_____

_____

Reflective Exercises

Exercise 1: Boundary Self-Assessment

Create a checklist of your boundaries, categorizing them into emotional, physical, and personal boundaries. Rate each boundary on a scale from 1 to 5 (1 being weak and 5 being strong) based on how effectively you currently maintain it. After evaluating, choose one boundary to focus on enhancing over the next month.

_____

_____

_____

Exercise 2: Active Listening Practicum

Pick a friend or family member to practice listening skills. Set aside some time to have a conversation where you focus on listening. Write in a journal about the experience: How did it feel to listen actively? What did you learn about your personal limits during this focused talk?

_____

_____

_____

_____

Exercise 3: Establishing Clear Expectations

Think about an area in your life where clear expectations could improve interactions—this could be at work, in friendships, or in family relationships. Outline these expectations clearly in writing, including examples of acceptable behavior. Share these expectations with the relevant parties and reflect on how the clarity impacts your relationships.

_____

_____

_____

_____

Exercise 4: Nonverbal Communication Check

Identify a scenario where you must verbally communicate a boundary. Write down your intended message and practice delivering it in front of a mirror. Pay attention to your body language, eye contact, and facial expressions. Afterward, write about how your nonverbal cues reinforced or contradicted your verbal message and how you can adjust them for clarity in real situations.

_____

_____

_____

Looking Ahead

As you work through these exercises, notice how your ability to set and maintain boundaries evolves. In the next chapter, we'll explore self-soothing techniques.

Final Reflection

What's your key takeaway from this chapter?

_____

_____

_____

What practice will you start with tomorrow?

_____

_____

_____

Your Personal Notes

Use this space for additional thoughts and insights:

_____

_____

CHAPTER 4:

Practicing Self-Soothing Techniques

Practicing self-soothing techniques plays a critical role in managing your emotional well-being. These methods provide us with the ability to navigate complex feelings, reduce anxiety, and maintain balance throughout our daily lives. You can address emotional fluctuations effectively by fostering self-regulation skills, ensuring a healthier mental state.

Such practices are especially beneficial for you as you strive to reparent your inner child, offering you tools to nurture and support yourself during challenging moments. The range of techniques available allows for personalized approaches, ensuring that you can find a method that resonates with you and fits seamlessly into your routine.

In this chapter, you will explore various mindfulness practices designed to enhance emotional regulation.

Quick Check-In Exercise

Before we explore self-soothing techniques, take a moment to check in with yourself:

Rate your current level (1–10):

- ❑ Ability to calm yourself when stressed: _____
- ❑ Awareness of your emotional state: _____
- ❑ Comfort with mindfulness practices: _____

What helps you feel calm right now?

_____

What tends to increase your stress?

_____

What self-soothing methods have you tried before?

_____

Exploring Mindfulness Practices

Because mindfulness techniques are so important, you will find we talk about them on more than one occasion. Enhancing emotional regulation through mindfulness is pivotal to nurturing one's mental health and overall well-being. Mindfulness practices provide valuable tools that help people ground themselves in the present moment, ultimately leading to greater emotional balance and tranquility. These practices include breath awareness, body scan techniques, mindful walking, and gratitude journaling. Each method contributes uniquely to emotional regulation, offering a path toward calmness and self-awareness.

Breath Awareness—A Fundamental Practice

Breath awareness provides immediate emotional regulation by anchoring individuals in the present moment. Engaging in breath awareness involves observing each inhalation and exhalation, which calms the mind and reduces anxiety. When overwhelmed by stress or racing thoughts, focusing on breathing can act as a powerful tool to bring you back to the here and now. This technique requires no special equipment or location—it's accessible at any moment, whether you're at your desk, waiting in line, or lying in bed. Regular practice of breath awareness fosters a more peaceful state of being, helping individuals remain centered during life's challenges (Mayo Clinic Staff, 2022).

Body Scan Technique

This is a technique that enhances the connection between mind and body, which is critical for identifying discomfort or tension stemming from past experiences. As you progress through the exercise, focus attention slowly on different parts of the body, acknowledging sensations without judgment. This mindful exploration raises awareness of physical discomfort and encourages acceptance of emotions linked to those feelings. The body scan allows individuals to become more attuned to their bodies, thus boosting self-awareness and fostering a holistic approach to emotional regulation (Ackerman, 2017).

Walking Mindfulness Into Motion

Mindful walking takes mindfulness into motion, integrating the practice into everyday activity. By being conscious of each step and the sensations experienced while walking, one can process emotions simultaneously, allowing them to dissipate instead of building up. Mindful walking offers dual benefits: it encourages the processing of complex emotions and promotes physical health, both essential for emotional well-being. Through this practice, individuals learn to observe their thoughts and emotions rather than become entangled in them while benefiting from physical exercise that reinforces resilience and vitality (Mayo Clinic Staff, 2022).

Journaling About Your Gratitude

Gratitude journaling acts as another potent tool for enhancing emotional resilience by shifting attention away from negativity and overwhelm. Individuals cultivate a positive mindset by regularly recording things they are thankful for, reinforcing emotional stability. This practice trains the brain to focus on positive aspects of life, counteracting the human tendency to dwell on negative experiences. Moreover, gratitude journaling nurtures an optimistic viewpoint, improving the overall sense of happiness and contentment. This positivity, in turn, strengthens emotional resilience, empowering individuals to face life's adversities with composure (Ackerman, 2017).

Implementation Guidelines Before You Start

Guidelines for implementing these mindfulness techniques effectively can enrich your practice.

- ❏ For breath awareness, find a quiet place where you won't be disturbed and sit comfortably. Close your eyes gently, breathe naturally, and direct your focus to the sensation of air entering and leaving your nostrils. Should your mind wander, kindly steer your attention back to your breath without reprimanding yourself.

- ❑ Activities like body scan meditation call for a dedicated space free from interruptions, ideally practiced daily to maximize benefits. Start by lying down and focusing on your toes, gradually moving your awareness up through your body to the crown of your head, tuning in to each sensation before moving to the next. Aim to practice this technique consistently, creating a routine that fits seamlessly into your daily life.

- ❑ Mindful walking can begin simply by slowing your pace and paying keen attention to every footfall. Whether walking down the street or pacing within your living room, focus on the rhythm of your steps, the feel of the ground beneath your feet, and the surrounding environment. Incorporate it into your routine by choosing a particular time or place to walk mindfully each day.

- ❑ With gratitude journaling, set aside a few minutes each evening to pen down three things you're grateful for, elaborating on why you appreciate them. Reflecting on these entries can elevate your mood and reinforce a positive outlook.

Interactive Exercise: Creating Your Calm Toolkit

Take a moment to identify and explore what brings you peace using different senses:

Visual Calm

- ❑ Colors that soothe me: _____
- ❑ Images that bring peace: _____
- ❑ Scenes that calm me: _____

Sound Serenity

- ❑ Calming sounds: _____
- ❑ Peaceful music: _____
- ❑ Soothing voices: _____

Touch Comfort

- ❑ Textures that soothe: _____
- ❑ Objects that comfort: _____
- ❑ Physical activities that calm: _____

Smell Safety

❑ Scents that relax me: _____

❑ Aromas that remind me of peace: _____

❑ Fragrances that ground me: _____

Taste Tranquility

❑ Flavors that comfort: _____

❑ Drinks that calm: _____

❑ Foods that soothe: _____

Now circle your top three most effective calming tools from any category above.

Visualization Techniques

Developing self-compassion and healing through visualization techniques provides individuals with powerful tools to manage emotions and improve their mental well-being. Visualization is a process where one creates vivid mental images to evoke sensory experiences. It can be an effective way to cultivate inner peace, resilience, and emotional balance. Let's explore how specific visualization practices can aid in emotional regulation and personal growth.

Safe Place Visualization

This involves creating a mental sanctuary, a retreat to which you can always return when you feel overwhelmed or stressed. This technique allows you to construct a haven tailored exclusively to your comfort and safety—a place where you can relax and heal emotionally.

Imagine a peaceful location, whether real or imagined, that brings you joy and tranquility. Perhaps it's a secluded beach, a quiet forest clearing, or a cozy room filled with soft light. As you visualize this space, employ all your senses: Envision the colors, listen to the sounds, and smell the air. The more details you incorporate, the more effective this visualization will be. You nurture a sense of security and trust within yourself by repeatedly visiting this safe place in your mind during difficult times. This practice helps reinforce your capacity for resilience and emotional protection (Visualization Meditation: 8 Exercises to Add to Your Practice, 2023).

Inner Child Visualization

This takes a step further by reconnecting with your younger self. This process encourages compassion and understanding toward past experiences that might still influence present emotions. Deep within, we all carry echoes of our childhood selves—hopes, feelings, and sometimes wounds we have yet to address.

Imagine meeting your inner child. Show them kindness, love, and acceptance. Have a comforting conversation, letting them know they are seen and heard. This nurturing experience can ease past pain and promote healing, allowing you to embrace your history while letting go of burdens. Inner child visualization reminds us that we can change our internal stories and treat ourselves with the kindness we deserve.

Healing Light Visualization

This technique utilizes the imagery of light as a symbol of strength and recovery. This method involves imagining a warm, radiant light enveloping your body, easing tension, and dispelling negativity.

Begin by visualizing this light entering from above, moving gently through each part of your body. As it progresses, any discomfort or stress dissolves under its soothing presence. Visualize the light healing not just physical ailments but emotional ones as well. This exercise reinforces relaxation, encouraging a state of empowerment and clarity when facing adversities. It's a way to remind yourself of your inherent ability to heal and cope effectively with life's challenges, promoting a sense of peace and renewal (Sutton, 2022).

Future Self Visualization

This is about envisioning a version of yourself that has evolved with grace and wisdom. In this practice, imagine meeting your future self—a person who embodies your aspirations and values. Picture them living a life imbued with fulfillment and happiness. What advice might they offer you? How have they overcome obstacles?

This visualization focuses on setting positive intentions, motivating you to take actionable steps toward becoming the person you wish to be. By maintaining a connection with this envisioned future self, you gain insight into your growth potential and develop a hopeful outlook. This practice inspires a continuous journey of self-compassion and improvement, reminding you that change is both possible and attainable.

More Practical Exercises

Let's explore some practical self-soothing techniques you can implement right away.

Diaphragmatic Breathing (Belly Breathing)

This technique helps to engage the diaphragm and encourages relaxation.

Steps:

1) Find a comfortable position, either sitting or lying down.

2) Place one hand on your chest and the other on your belly.

3) Inhale deeply through your nose, allowing your belly to rise while keeping your chest relatively still.

4) Exhale slowly through your mouth, feeling your belly fall.

5) Continue this for 5–10 minutes, focusing on the rise and fall of your belly.

Reflection Prompt

How did this exercise make you feel? Did you notice any changes in your anxiety or stress levels?

_____

_____

The 4-7-8 Breathing

This technique is excellent for reducing anxiety and promoting relaxation.

Steps:

1) Sit or lie down comfortably.

2) Close your eyes and take a deep breath through your nose for a count of 4.

3) Hold your breath for a count of 7.

4) Exhale slowly through your mouth for a count of 8, making a whooshing sound.

5) Repeat this cycle for 4–6 breaths.

Reflection Prompt

What sensations did you experience during this exercise? Did it help clear your mind or calm your body?

_____

_____

Box Breathing

This exercise is great for instilling a feeling of calm and focus.

Steps:

- ❑ Sit in a comfortable position and close your eyes.
- ❑ Inhale deeply through your nose for a count of 4.
- ❑ Hold your breath for a count of 4.
- ❑ Exhale slowly through your mouth for a count of 4.
- ❑ Hold your breath again for a count of 4.
- ❑ Repeat this cycle for 5–10 minutes.

Reflection Prompt

How did this structured breathing pattern affect your thoughts and feelings? Were you able to maintain your focus throughout?

_____

_____

Alternate Nostril Breathing (Nadi Shodhana)

This technique promotes balance and relaxation by harmonizing the right and left hemispheres of the brain.

Steps:

- ❑ Sit comfortably with your spine straight.
- ❑ Use your right thumb to close your right nostril.

- ❑ Inhale deeply through your left nostril.
- ❑ Close your left nostril with your right ring finger and release your thumb from your right nostril.
- ❑ Exhale through the right nostril.
- ❑ Inhale through the right nostril, then close it again with your thumb.
- ❑ Release your left nostril and exhale through it.
- ❑ Continue alternating nostrils for 5–10 cycles.

Reflection Prompt

How did this exercise impact your sense of calm or mental clarity? Did you notice any physical sensations during the practice?

_____

_____

Incorporating these practical breathing exercises into your daily routine can help enhance your self-soothing toolkit. Reflecting on your experiences after each exercise will deepen your understanding of how each technique affects your emotional state and overall well-being.

Journaling Prompts

Prompt 1: Reflecting on Emotional Fluctuations

Spend a moment reflecting on a recent emotional experience that felt overwhelming. Describe the situation in detail. How did you respond? Which self-soothing techniques could you have employed at that moment? Write about how you felt before and after trying these techniques.

_____

_____

Prompt 2: Breath Awareness Practice

After experiencing a moment of anxiety or stress, describe your experience with breath awareness. Note how focusing on your breath affected your emotional state. What sensations did you notice in your body? How did your feelings change as you engaged in this practice?

___

___

___

___

Prompt 3: Safe Place Visualization

Visualize your safe place and write about your experience. Describe the elements of this place—what do you see, hear, and feel? How does being in this safe space make you feel emotionally and physically? Reflect on how you can access this safe place during challenging times.

___

___

___

___

Reflective Exercises

Exercise 1: Body Scan Awareness

Commit to practicing a body scan technique once a week for the next month. During each session, note the sensations you experience in different parts of your body. After each practice, write down your experience in a journal: What did you discover about areas of tension or discomfort? How did your feelings shift during the exercise?

___

___

___

___

Exercise 2: Mindful Walking Experience

Choose a time to engage in mindful walking for the next month at least once a week. During your walks, focus on your steps and surroundings. After each walk, reflect in your journal: How did the practice influence your emotional state? Did you notice any shifts in your thoughts or feelings?

_____

_____

_____

Exercise 3: Inner Child Visualization

Allocate a quiet moment to visualize your inner child. Describe this visualization in your journal: What does your inner child look like? How do you feel interacting with them? Write about the dialogue you had: what support or comfort did you provide during this visualization?

_____

_____

_____

Exercise 4: Future Self Visualization

Write about the version of you that you envision for the future. What qualities do they possess? What accomplishments have they achieved? In what ways do they demonstrate self-compassion? Reflect on practical steps you can take now to start working toward this future self.

_____

_____

_____

Looking Ahead

As you work through these exercises, notice how your ability to self-soothe evolves. In the next chapter, we'll discuss how to create a safe emotional environment.

Final Reflection

What's your key takeaway from this chapter?

_____

_____

_____

_____

What practice will you start with tomorrow?

_____

_____

_____

_____

Your Personal Notes

Use this space for additional thoughts and insights:

_____

_____

_____

_____

_____

_____

_____

_____

CHAPTER 5:

Creating a Safe Emotional Environment

Creating a safe emotional environment is an endeavor that touches upon every aspect of your everyday interactions. It isn't merely about finding comfort zones; it's about establishing spaces where you feel empowered to be your true self without fearing judgment or negative repercussions. A conducive atmosphere allows for authentic expression and personal growth, fostering a deeper understanding of yourself and others. By crafting such supportive environments, you can navigate your emotions more effectively, building resilience and emotional intelligence in the process.

This chapter investigates the importance of these emotional havens and their impact on your personal development. We'll discuss ways to identify harmful influences and behaviors that affect your emotions.

Emotional Safety and Recognizing Supportive Environments

Creating a safe emotional environment is key to your personal development and the establishment of supportive surroundings that encourage continuous emotional growth. The significance of feeling emotionally safe lies in providing you with a space where you can be open, vulnerable, and authentic without fear of judgment or rejection. To achieve this, it is essential for you to identify toxic influences, evaluate your relationships, cultivate positive spaces, and practice emotional expression.

Recognizing Toxic Influences

This involves understanding the patterns, behaviors, and characteristics that contribute to emotional instability. It is imperative to be aware of environments that encourage negative emotions, such as criticism, manipulation, or inconsistency, which can undermine one's sense of security. When you identify these detrimental elements, you can take deliberate steps to distance yourself from harmful influences and seek healthier alternatives.

Develop Criteria for Healthy Connections

Developing criteria for evaluating relationships assists in determining which connections support emotional safety and stability. Establishing standards helps in discerning relationships that offer empathy, respect, and understanding. Prioritizing qualities like trustworthiness, honesty, and mutual respect can guide individuals in making informed choices about the people they associate with. This process also involves assessing whether relationships provide a balance of give-and-take, ensuring both parties feel valued and heard.

Cultivating Positive Spaces

This is about implementing changes to create comforting atmospheres that prioritize your self-care and emotional health. This involves organizing your physical environment and emotional surroundings in ways that enhance your well-being. Creating spaces filled with positivity and comfort impacts how you process your emotions and interact with others. Incorporating self-care practices into your daily routine, such as mindfulness or meditation, can strengthen your emotional resilience and promote inner peace.

Implementing guidelines to establish emotionally healthy spaces includes setting boundaries, fostering open dialogue, and encouraging personal growth. Practice active listening and empathy to understand others' perspectives and validate their emotions. Building an emotionally supportive space requires ongoing attention and effort, as it involves adapting to changes in your relationships and environments. Such spaces are beneficial for your personal growth and contribute to the collective well-being of those involved.

Practicing Emotional Expression

This emphasizes safely sharing feelings by understanding the impact of vulnerability and enhancing communication. Being open about emotions is fundamental to developing strong interpersonal connections, as it enables individuals to express needs and desires without fear. Encouraging open communication within relationships can lead to deeper understanding and trust, forming the foundation for lasting bonds.

To effectively share feelings, one must recognize the role vulnerability plays in building emotional connections. Vulnerability fosters intimacy and fosters a sense of shared humanity, breaking down barriers between individuals. When expressing oneself, it is vital to articulate thoughts and emotions clearly while also being receptive to others' experiences. This exchange nurtures a culture of mutual respect and understanding, which is essential for fostering emotionally safe environments.

The process of creating a safe emotional environment necessitates continuous reflection and adaptation. As you grow and change, so do your emotional needs and the dynamics of your surroundings. Regularly assessing the state of your emotional environment ensures it remains conducive to growth and well-being. This ongoing evaluation allows you to fine-tune their strategies and make necessary adjustments to maintain emotional safety.

Building Supportive Relationships and Community Networks

Surrounding yourself with nurturing and supportive relationships plays a vital role in facilitating emotional growth.

Intimate and communal relationships are key to fostering environments where individuals feel safe to express themselves and grow. Through these connections, people can build resilience against life's challenges and experience profound personal development.

Identifying Supportive Persons

This is the first step toward building an emotionally enriching environment. You need to distinguish between relationships that uplift you and those that drain you. Supportive individuals typically show traits like empathy, reliability, trustworthiness, and positivity. They listen to you and contribute to your sense of self-worth and security. By recognizing these qualities, you can discern which relationships are beneficial and which may be harmful.

Understanding the difference is necessary because some interactions might seem supportive on the surface but may contain underlying negativity that stifles your emotional growth. Family and friends play key roles in this area. They are often the foundation of your emotional safety and provide unique insights into understanding these dynamics.

Nurturing Connections Through Intentional Effort

Key practices include active listening, sharing mutual interests, and engaging in activities that promote a shared sense of accomplishment.

- ❏ Listen actively: This involves more than just hearing words; you must fully engage with what the other person says and responding thoughtfully.

- ❏ Show empathy: This entails understanding another's feelings and perspectives, is equally important. These skills help deepen bonds and create spaces where emotional truths can be shared openly.

- ❏ Share experiences: Doing things together like exercise, creative endeavors, or even simple leisure activities can strengthen these ties further and contribute to well-being. Such engagements fulfill our innate need for connection and enhance emotional resilience and joy. Research suggests that healthy friendships have a huge impact on mental health by offering support and creating a sense of belonging (Strong Relationships, Strong Health, 2022).

- ❏ Boundary setting: Establishing relational boundaries safeguards emotional health. It involves clearly defining personal limits to protect your well-being within relationships. This means knowing when to say no, recognizing personal needs, and communicating them effectively.

- ❏ Assertive communication: These techniques are invaluable here; they ensure that conflicts are addressed respectfully and constructively without compromising personal values. Establishing boundaries also helps identify when a relationship becomes detrimental. Although challenging, letting go of harmful connections is sometimes necessary for maintaining emotional balance. Such decisions require careful evaluation of how different interactions affect one's mental state and the courage to prioritize health over comfort.

- ❏ Developing collective strength: Fostering community adds another dimension to emotional growth. Building a network of supportive individuals who share common goals or interests offers collective strength. Whether through group activities, support groups, or community initiatives, shared experiences foster a sense of unity and encouragement. These groups act as buffers against isolation and provide opportunities for mutual support and inspiration. Participating in community activities enhances social interactions and contributes to individual development by exposing one to diverse perspectives and experiences. Environments where encouragement and empathy are prevalent nurture emotional growth and foster a stronger sense of belonging.

The benefits of nurturing supportive relationships extend beyond personal gains. They positively impact broader society by promoting healthier communities where collaboration and understanding thrive.

People engaged in strong, supportive networks tend to contribute more positively to their surroundings, reflecting the value of emotionally enriched relationships in societal contexts. Some research underscores the significance of positive relationships in enhancing mental health and overall well-being (Strong Relationships, Strong Health, 2022).

More Interactive Exercises

Explore a variety of engaging exercises designed to reconnect with and nurture your inner child throughout this workbook.

Journaling Prompts

Prompt 1: Identifying Emotional Safety

Reflect on your current emotional surroundings. Journal about when you felt completely safe expressing your feelings and thoughts. What factors contributed to this sense of safety? Describe the qualities of that environment and the people involved. How can you replicate these elements in your current life?

_____

_____

_____

Prompt 2: Recognizing Toxic Influences

Write about any relationships or environments that feel draining or harmful. Identify specific behaviors or patterns within these situations that lead to feelings of anxiety or discomfort. What steps can you take to protect yourself from these influences? Consider ways to distance yourself or set boundaries in these relationships.

_____

_____

_____

Prompt 3: Cultivating Positive Spaces

Describe what a positive emotional environment looks like for you. List three specific actions you can take to enhance your current surroundings (e.g., decluttering your space, adding comforting items, or creating routines) that prioritize self-care. How do you envision these changes impacting your emotional well-being?

_____

_____

_____

Prompt 4: Practicing Emotional Expression

Journal about a recent experience where you struggled to express your feelings. What emotions were you feeling, and what held you back from sharing them? Describe how articulating these feelings could strengthen your relationships. Write down strategies or techniques you can use moving forward to communicate more openly with others.

_____

_____

_____

Reflective Exercises

Activity 1: Mapping Your Support System

Sketch a support system map. In the center, write your name; around it, list individuals who uplift and support you. Note their qualities that contribute to your emotional safety (like empathy or reliability). Reflect on how you can further nurture these relationships. What small steps can you take to strengthen your connections with these individuals?

_____

_____

_____

_____

Activity 2: Boundary Setting Guide

Reflect on a situation where you felt your boundaries were challenged. Journal about what happened and how it made you feel. Write down an assertive boundary statement you could use in the future to protect your emotional space. What steps will you take to communicate this boundary effectively, and how do you feel about asserting your needs?

___

___

___

Activities to Develop Community and Connection

Activity 1: Creating Connections

Think about a community group or activity that interests you (like a hobby group, volunteer opportunity, or support group). Write about why this group appeals to you and how it aligns with your values. Outline steps for how you will engage with this community, including any barriers you might face and how to overcome them.

___

___

Activity 2: Empathy Practice

Choose a friend or family member with whom you'd like to connect more deeply. Prepare for a conversation where you practice active listening and empathy. Write a plan that details:

- ❑ What topics will you discuss to create a space for open dialogue?

- ❑ How you will demonstrate active listening (e.g., summarizing what they say, asking clarifying questions).

- ❑ Reflect after the conversation on what you learned about them and how this practice contributed to strengthening your emotional connection.

___

___

In this chapter, we've explored the essentials of creating a supportive environment that nurtures continuous emotional growth.

Let's move on to the Conclusion, where we'll recap what we've learned.

CONCLUSION

As we reach the end of our journey together through the phases of inner child healing, it's essential to reflect on the life-changing power of embracing our inner child.

The path to healing begins with acknowledging and nurturing our inner child, the forgotten part of ourselves yearning for attention and care. Connecting with this inner child unlocks joy and creativity, often lost in adulthood's responsibilities. This isn't just nostalgia; it's essential for personal growth and emotional healing.

When you accept your inner child, you regain the playful spirit that once defined you. Nurturing this aspect heals past wounds and revitalizes the present, allowing us to face the world with renewed vigor. The journey of reparenting requires us to honor our needs with compassion and patience.

Self-compassion is central to healing. In a society that equates self-worth with productivity, practicing self-kindness is radical. Acknowledging your humanity builds emotional resilience, helping you manage life's storms with grace. Embracing self-compassion enhances our relationships, developing empathy and understanding.

Establishing healthy boundaries in adult life safeguards your emotional well-being. These boundaries ensure clear communication of your needs and prevent overwhelm. They are bridges to deeper connections based on mutual respect.

Creating a safe emotional environment promotes personal growth. Surrounding ourselves with supportive people nurtures our desires and dreams, providing a sanctuary for exploration.

Healing our inner child is a shared experience, strengthening community bonds. As we celebrate each victory, we honor the courage it takes to embark on this journey. Embrace your inner child, trust the healing process, and let self-compassion guide you.

If you've enjoyed this workbook, join us again in *Workbook 3: Emotional Healing Workbook—Step-by-Step Guidance to Release Pain, Overcome Self-Sabotage, and Find Lasting Freedom* to continue your personal development journey.

BOOK 3

Emotional Healing Workbook

Step-by-Step Guidance to Release Pain, Overcome Self-Sabotage, and Find Lasting Freedom

INTRODUCTION

Have you ever felt trapped in a cycle of self-defeat, questioning why certain obstacles keep reappearing in your life? You might sense the weight of past traumas hindering your potential or recognize recurring behavior patterns that sabotage your efforts before you can even begin.

Many adults share this struggle as they search for personal growth and emotional healing. Self-sabotage, often an invisible hurdle, can obstruct both progress and inner peace. This book aspires to be a guiding light for those ready to liberate themselves from self-imposed limitations, offering practical tools and insights to help overcome entrenched emotional pain and unproductive habits.

This life-changing process starts with the critical step of identifying the specific triggers that lead to your self-destructive tendencies. It is essential to understand the particular situations, individuals, or emotional states that evoke negative reactions. By cultivating this awareness, you empower yourself to observe your thoughts and feelings without judgment, enabling you to choose healthier responses.

Think of this process as mapping potential pitfalls on a road trip; recognizing where obstacles exist equips you to navigate them with poise and intention. After pinpointing these triggers, the next phase involves replacing unhelpful patterns with constructive alternatives. Imagine revamping your mental landscape by removing the debris of old habits and establishing a strong foundation for new, supportive behaviors. Together, we will delve into common self-destructive tendencies—like procrastination, self-criticism, and avoidance—normalizing these experiences to alleviate feelings of shame and isolation.

With a greater understanding of your behaviors, you'll explore strategies aimed at substituting harmful habits with practical steps to encourage different responses during challenging moments. When you commit to intentional decision-making, you embrace empowerment, while practicing alternative behaviors solidifies positive changes and enhances mental well-being.

Creating a personal action plan is necessary in your quest to conquer self-sabotage. Think of this plan as a roadmap—a written guide that translates dreams into tangible goals. By establishing clear objectives, you'll not only track your progress but also maintain accountability to yourself. Documenting your commitments reinforces your dedication to personal growth and healing.

The journey to emotional freedom is seldom traveled alone. Highlighting the importance of accountability can bolster your resolve. This book will discuss the concept of accountability partners—trustworthy allies who share your aspirations and motivate you to stay committed.

Regular check-ins will help keep your goals forefront in your mind, allowing space for reflection on accomplishments and challenges alike. Envision a future unencumbered by past traumas, a life where you can chase your dreams devoid of doubt and fear. This book serves as a guide and an invitation for you to reclaim your story and empower your capacity for change.

Within this workbook, you will learn to process painful memories, release guilt and shame, and understand self-sabotaging behaviors. You will discover techniques to rewrite limiting beliefs rooted in childhood and cultivate emotional freedom and peace.

In this workbook you'll discover how to process pain and move on to an emotionally free future:

1) **Processing Painful Childhood Memories**

2) **Techniques for Letting Go of Guilt, Shame, and Resentment**

3) **Understanding and Overcoming Self-Sabotaging Behaviors**

4) **Rewriting Limiting Beliefs Rooted in Childhood**

5) **Building Emotional Freedom and Peace**

Our objective is to equip you with practical exercises that support emotional release, enabling you to confront and heal from ingrained pain. Through a combination of empathy, encouragement, and evidence-based practices, this user-friendly resource aims to resonate with your personal experiences and ambitions.

Together, let's begin this expedition toward emotional liberation and resilience, exploring avenues that foster self-understanding and lasting fulfillment.

CHAPTER 1:

Processing Painful Childhood Memories

Looking back at your past, you can uncover feelings that still impact your life today, shaping how you interact with others and make choices. This process is not about reliving past pain but recognizing how it has influenced who you are now. In this chapter, you will look at the causes of the emotional patterns from your childhood.

Processing painful childhood memories involves a series of intentional steps that allow you to confront and work through these experiences, ultimately leading to healing and self-discovery. We'll explore them in this chapter.

Quick Check-In Exercise

Before we explore painful childhood memories, take a moment to check in with yourself:

Rate your current level (1–10):

❑ Emotional readiness to explore memories: _____

❑ Current feeling of safety: _____

❑ Access to support systems: _____

How are you feeling about this exploration?

_____

What support do you need right now?

_____

What helps you feel grounded when emotions arise?

_____

_____

_____

Remember: You can take breaks or step away at any time during this process.

Understanding the Impact of Trauma, Neglect, and Unmet Needs on Emotional Patterns

Reflecting on how your past, particularly experiences of trauma, neglect, and unmet needs, influences your present is a large part of your healing journey. These early experiences can create lasting emotional patterns that shape your reactions and relationships as an adult. Understanding these patterns is vital to promoting emotional well-being and fostering personal growth.

Some examples include:

- ❑ A child who grew up in a household where their emotional needs were often overlooked may develop challenges in trusting others as adults, frequently isolating themselves to avoid the pain of potential rejection.

- ❑ An individual who experienced minimal attention and support during their formative years may carry deep-seated fears of abandonment into their adult life, leading to patterns of pushing loved ones away despite wanting closeness.

- ❑ When a person encounters neglect during their early developmental stages, they might grapple with profound trust issues in their later relationships, commonly withdrawing from connections to shield themselves from being hurt.

Your thoughts:

_____

_____

_____

_____

Identifying Emotional Responses Linked to Trauma and Neglect

Trauma and neglect often give rise to emotional triggers that can impact how you interact with the world. For example, if you experienced neglect or inconsistent caregiving in childhood, you might find yourself overly sensitive to perceived rejection or criticism as an adult. This heightened sensitivity could lead to intense emotional responses that others may perceive as overreactions, often rooted in those early painful experiences.

Some examples include:

- ❑ A person who experienced inconsistent caregiving; they might display extreme jealousy in their relationships, stemming from the fear of being abandoned, resulting in emotional outbursts when their partner interacts with others.

- ❑ Someone who faced emotional neglect during childhood, leading them to feel abandoned when their partner doesn't respond immediately to a text message. This can escalate into feelings of worthlessness and anxiety, causing them to lash out.

- ❑ An individual who was bullied as a child; as an adult, they may have disproportionate reactions to criticism at work, perceiving it as a personal attack rather than constructive feedback, which can hinder their professional growth and relationships.

These reactions stem from the adaptive strategies you developed in response to threats during your formative years, but they may no longer be effective in a safe environment.

Your thoughts:

_____

_____

_____

_____

Guided Visualization for Comforting the Inner Child

A powerful way to process painful memories and reconnect with your inner child is through guided visualization. This exercise allows you to create a safe space in your mind to revisit past experiences with compassion and care. Follow these easy steps:

1) 1. Find a quiet, comfortable space where you can relax without interruptions.

2) 2. Close your eyes and take a few deep breaths, allowing yourself to center and calm your mind.

3) 3. Imagine a safe and comforting setting, such as a serene beach or a cozy room filled with soft light.

4) 4. Visualize your younger self in this space. Notice how they look and feel. What emotions do you sense from them?

5) 5. As you engage with your inner child, offer them reassurance, love, and acceptance. Speak kindly to them, acknowledging their feelings and experiences.

6) 6. Allow your inner child to express their emotions while you listen attentively. Validate their feelings and provide comfort.

7) 7. After a few moments, visualize wrapping your younger self in a gentle hug, reinforcing that they are safe and loved.

8) 8. Gradually bring your awareness back to the present, taking deep breaths before opening your eyes.

After the visualization, take a moment to journal about your experience. Write down any insights, emotions, or messages you received from your inner child during the exercise.

_____

_____

_____

_____

_____

Creative Healing Methods

In addition to guided visualization, exploring creative healing methods can enhance your journey toward processing painful memories.

1) **Art therapy:** Create an art piece that represents your feelings about a particular memory. Use colors, shapes, or imagery that resonates with you. This visual expression can help release emotions and provide clarity.

2) **Movement-based healing:** Engage in a movement practice, such as dancing, yoga, or walking, allowing your body to express the emotions you've traced back to childhood trauma. Focus on how movement helps release tension and reconnects you with your feelings.

3) **Voice-recorded messages to your inner child:** Use your phone or a recording device to record a message to your inner child. Speak from your adult perspective, offering comfort, understanding, and assurance.

Keeping a Trigger Journal

While this chapter focuses on various techniques for healing, the practice of journaling remains a valuable tool for reflecting on patterns in your emotional responses. This serves as a reminder to write down instances that trigger strong emotions, to help you see recurring themes. Each entry allows you to reflect and learn, gradually uncovering connections to your early experiences. This practice promotes personal growth and fosters a compassionate understanding of your behaviors.

Interactive Exercise: Creating Your Safety Plan

Before diving into memory work, let's establish your emotional safety net:

Grounding Tools

- ❑ Three things I can see right now: _____
- ❑ Three things I can touch: _____
- ❑ Three things I can hear: _____

My Support System

- ❑ Trusted friend/family member to call: _____
- ❑ Professional support available: _____
- ❑ Safe places I can go: _____

Self-Care Strategies

- ❑ Activities that calm me: _____
- ❑ Things that bring comfort: _____
- ❑ Ways to self-soothe: _____

Emergency Resources

☐ Therapist/counselor contact: _____

☐ Crisis hotline number: _____

☐ Safe person to reach out to: _____

Check in with yourself after completing this plan

☐ How do I feel now? _____

☐ What else do I need? _____

☐ Am I ready to proceed? _____

More Practical Exercises

Explore a variety of engaging exercises designed to reconnect with and nurture your inner child throughout this workbook.

Creative Healing Methods

Activity 1: Guided Visualization for Your Inner Child

☐ Set aside quiet time for a guided visualization. Close your eyes and imagine meeting your inner child in a safe, comforting space.

☐ Describe what your inner child looks like, their emotions, and what they need from you.

☐ Write down the insights or messages you received during this visualization. How can you take actions in your daily life to honor these needs?

_____

_____

Activity 2: Art Therapy Exploration

☐ Create an art piece that represents a painful memory or feeling. Use colors, shapes, and materials that resonate with your emotions.

- ❑ After completing the piece, reflect on the experience. What did the process reveal to you about your feelings toward that memory?

_____
_____
_____
_____

Activity 3: Movement-Based Healing

- ❑ Engage in a physical activity that allows you to express emotions tied to your childhood. This could be dance, yoga, or even a walk in nature, focusing on how your body feels during each movement.

- ❑ Afterward, journal about how the movement helped you release or connect with emotions linked to your past.

_____
_____
_____
_____

Activity 4: Voice-Recorded Letter to Your Inner Child

- ❑ Use a recording device on your phone to send a message to your inner child. Speak naturally, offering comfort and understanding for their pain.

- ❑ After recording, listen to the message. Reflect on how it feels to acknowledge and communicate with your inner child in this way.

_____
_____
_____
_____

Reflection Prompts

Prompt 1: Memory Retrieval Reflection

Choose a painful memory from your childhood. Write a detailed narrative describing the event, including the sights, sounds, emotions, and people involved. After recounting the memory, how has this event shaped your current emotional responses? What specific patterns or behaviors do you recognize in yourself today that may be linked to this memory?

_____

_____

_____

Prompt 2: Safety and Support Reflection

Reflect on times during your childhood when you felt supported and safe. Write about these moments and the people who provided that support. How can you channel the feelings of safety and support from those memories into your present life? What steps can you take to create a safe space for yourself now?

_____

_____

_____

Engaging With Your Inner Child

Activity 1: Inner Child Visualization Session

Set aside quiet time for a guided visualization. Close your eyes and imagine meeting your inner child in a safe, comforting space. Describe what your inner child looks like, their emotions, and what they need from you. Write down the insights or messages you received during this visualization. How can you take actions in your daily life to honor these needs?

_____

_____

_____

Activity 2: Create a Joyful Activity List

Reflect on activities you enjoyed as a child. Create a list of these joyful pursuits and commit to incorporating at least one into your weekly routine. Write a journal entry about what it felt like to engage in these activities and how it affected your overall mood and connection with your inner child.

_____

_____

_____

Developing Compassion and Forgiveness

Write a letter to your younger self expressing compassion and understanding for the pain they felt. Acknowledge their feelings, offer words of kindness, and assure them that they are loved and cared for. Reflect on how writing this letter impacts your understanding of your past experiences and how it fosters forgiveness.

_____

_____

Looking Ahead

As you work through these exercises, notice how your relationship with these memories evolves. In the next chapter, we'll explore techniques for letting go of guilt, shame, and resentment.

Final Reflection

What's your key takeaway from this chapter?

_____

_____

What practice will you start with tomorrow?

_____

_____

Your Personal Notes

Use this space for additional thoughts and insights:

CHAPTER 2:

Techniques for Letting Go of Guilt, Shame and Resentment

Letting go of guilt, shame, and resentment can free you emotionally. These feelings often tie you to the past, making it hard to move forward and grow. Many people get stuck, unable to release old grievances or mistakes, which can lead to constant self-blame and unhappiness.

Understanding the burden these emotions create is the first step to freeing yourself, allowing you to find effective ways to let them go. By starting this journey, you can free yourself from these weights and open up space for more positive experiences. This chapter presents methods and exercises to help you release heavy emotions.

Quick Check-In Exercise

Before we explore letting go of difficult emotions, take a moment to check in with yourself:

Rate your current level (1–10):

❑ Awareness of these emotions: _____

❑ Readiness to release them: _____

❑ Self-compassion practice: _____

Which emotion feels strongest right now?

_____

Where do you feel it in your body?

_____

What would letting go feel like?

___

Practice Forgiveness Toward Self and Others

Forgiveness is a powerful and transformative process often misunderstood as excusing an offense. In reality, it's about freeing yourself from the heavy burden of resentment and anger. At its core, forgiveness is a conscious decision to release these emotional weights, allowing you to find inner peace and emotional liberation. This act offers a pathway to healing, enabling you to move forward with renewed strength and clarity.

Understanding Forgiveness

Forgiveness begins by recognizing it as a gift you give yourself rather than an endorsement of wrongdoing. By choosing forgiveness, you create space for growth and transformation. This liberating choice allows you to break free from the cycle of bitterness that can hold you back from experiencing joy and fulfillment. When you let go of past grievances, you empower yourself to live in the present moment, unencumbered by past pains.

Self-Forgiveness

One of the most important aspects of forgiveness is self-forgiveness, a practice often overlooked but significant for your emotional health. Self-forgiveness involves acknowledging your mistakes, understanding that error is a natural part of being human, and engaging in self-reflection to learn and grow. It requires embracing your imperfections with compassion. Reflective practices, such as journaling or meditative exercises, offer avenues for this introspection, helping you to process emotions and foster self-compassion.

Key Steps to Self-Forgiveness

A practical way to begin forgiving yourself involves several key steps.

1) First, acknowledge your mistake without self-judgment.
2) Recognizing your errors honestly and courageously is the groundwork for self-acceptance.

3) Understanding the context in which mistakes occurred—considering factors like stress or external pressures—can provide insight into their occurrence.

4) Taking responsibility is key; it shifts the focus from blame and excuses to accountability, fostering personal growth.

5) Finally, showing yourself compassion and learning from the experience are vital to moving beyond guilt and shame toward self-betterment.

Forgiving Others

When you forgive others, an important release of emotions happens within you. Holding onto grudges only perpetuates pain, whereas releasing them opens up avenues for healing. Practical steps for forgiving others may involve verbalizing forgiveness, either through writing in a journal or speaking directly with the individual involved. These processes can enhance your personal peace and promote healthier relationships.

The Power of Writing

Expressing forgiveness in writing, such as composing a forgiveness letter, can be profoundly cathartic for you. It provides a structured opportunity to articulate feelings, offering clarity and closure. A decision-based intervention proposed by McCullough and Worthington (1995) involves drafting such a letter, enabling you to initiate forgiveness and continue the work independently. The act of explicitly stating your intent to forgive helps in processing complex emotions and untangling yourself from past hurt.

The REACH Model

This is a forgiveness model developed by Dr E. Worthington (Wade et al., 2014), which is another effective strategy, providing a structured approach to forgiving others. It guides you through recalling the hurt, developing empathy, reframing forgiveness as an altruistic act, committing to forgive, and holding onto that forgiveness. Each step encourages your personal reflection and emotional connection, making forgiveness more attainable.

Developing Empathy

Developing empathy for others' perspectives is a key element of forgiveness for you. It involves understanding the motives and circumstances behind the actions that caused harm. This understanding fosters a sense of compassion and reduces the intensity of negative emotions. Techniques such as guided imagery or visualizations can aid in cultivating empathy, encouraging a broader perspective on interpersonal conflicts.

The Broader Impact of Forgiveness

While the journey of forgiveness is deeply personal, its effects extend beyond yourself. Those who practice forgiveness often report improved mental health, reduced stress, and stronger relationships. The positive ripple effect of forgiving yourself and others enhances not only your personal well-being but also the well-being of those around you. As your capacity for forgiveness expands, it fosters an environment of understanding and compassion in interpersonal connections.

Honoring Your Journey

It is important to note that forgiveness does not always imply reconciliation, nor does it require forgetting the transgression. Instead, it marks a decision to move past the pain and embrace positivity. For some, especially those who have experienced severe trauma, forgiveness might not be immediately possible or even desirable. You must approach this process at your own pace and discretion, honoring your unique experiences and boundaries.

Interactive Exercise: Emotional Release Inventory

Take a moment to map out what you're ready to release:

Guilt Inventory

- ❑ What I feel guilty about: _____

- ❑ Why I've held onto this: _____

- ❑ What releasing it would mean: _____

Shame Inventory

- ❑ What brings up shame: _____

- ❑ Messages I received about this: _____

- ❑ New perspective I'm choosing: _____

Resentment Inventory

- ❑ Who/what I resent: _____
- ❑ How it affects me: _____
- ❑ What freedom would feel like: _____

Choose one item from above to focus on today:

- ❑ I choose to work with: _____
- ❑ First small step I can take: _____
- ❑ Support I need: _____

Use Mindfulness to Detach from Negative Emotions

You've already learned that mindfulness is a powerful tool. Now, let's use it for observing and releasing intense emotions such as guilt, shame, and resentment. Mindfulness practices encourage you to focus on the present moment, reducing your inclination to judge or dwell on negative feelings. This process of staying aware without judgment not only calms your mind but also enhances your understanding of your emotional landscape. Cultivating this kind of awareness creates an environment conducive to emotional release.

Mindful Breathing

Breathing techniques help alleviate emotional tension and interrupt cycles of negative thoughts. For example, a simple exercise involves taking deep, rhythmic breaths—inhale deeply through your nose for a count of four, hold the breath for a second, and then exhale slowly through your mouth to a count of five. This practice helps steady your mind and offers a way to detach from overwhelming emotions. Repeatedly engaging in such exercises can foster a more profound sense of calm and presence, ultimately helping you manage your intense feelings.

Body Scan Meditation

This method aids in recognizing how emotions manifest physically in your body, often as tension or discomfort. During a body scan, you lie down comfortably and direct attention to each part of your body sequentially, from toes to head or vice versa. The key is to notice any sensations without trying to change them. This practice is about cultivating an awareness of where emotions might reside physically and understanding their connection to your mental states. Regularly practicing body scans helps you develop a better awareness of how stress or resentment affects your physical well-being.

Journaling

Beyond these practices, journaling serves as an excellent tool for mindfulness and emotional clarity for you. Through mindful reflection in writing, you can begin to discern patterns and emotional triggers, gaining insights that aren't always apparent in the hustle of daily life. Journaling provides a structured way to process emotions by offering clarity and perspective. By noting down your thoughts and experiences, you gain the ability to observe recurring themes and reactions, thus identifying areas needing emotional attention or healing. Engaging with this reflective practice helps solidify the habit of being present and receptive to what emotions reveal about your experiences and growth opportunities.

Being Consistent in Your Approach

Mindfulness, when integrated into your daily life routines, supports emotional release by fostering a compassionate and non-judgmental relationship with yourself. It requires dedication and practice, but the rewards can be transformative for you. Slowly but surely, it becomes easier to navigate through heavy emotions, responding with greater acceptance and less resistance. Each practice of mindfulness, be it through breathing, a body scan, or journaling, acts as a stepping stone toward emotional liberation. By engaging regularly with these techniques, you learn to relate differently to your thoughts and feelings, reducing the grip of guilt, shame, and resentment over time.

Mindfulness is not about being perfect in managing your emotions but about being aware and accepting of yourself. As you practice mindfulness regularly, your feelings of guilt and resentment start to change. They don't disappear instantly, but they become less powerful as you recognize them as temporary feelings rather than who you are.

More Practical Exercises

Explore a variety of engaging exercises designed to reconnect with and nurture your inner child throughout this workbook.

Letter-Writing Activities

Activity 1: Letter of Forgiveness to Yourself

- ❏ Write a letter to yourself expressing forgiveness for past mistakes or regrets.
- ❏ Acknowledge the emotions of guilt and shame you've been holding onto.
- ❏ Offer words of compassion and understanding, recognizing that making mistakes is part of being human.
- ❏ Conclude the letter with a commitment to treat yourself with kindness and to learn from these experiences rather than be defined by them.

_____

_____

_____

_____

_____

Activity 2: Letter of Forgiveness to Others

- ❏ Draft a letter to someone you feel resentment toward.
- ❏ In this letter, express your feelings honestly, but aim for a tone of forgiveness.
- ❏ Explain how their actions affected you and the emotional weight you've been carrying.
- ❏ State your intention to release these feelings and let go of the resentment. This letter can be kept private or shared, depending on your feelings.

_____

_____

_____

_____

_____

Mindfulness Practices for Emotional Release

Activity 1: Compassion-Focused Meditation

- ❑ Set aside 10–15 minutes in a quiet space. Close your eyes and take deep breaths to center yourself.

- ❑ Begin by bringing to mind a memory that evokes feelings of guilt or shame.

- ❑ Visualize your younger self affected by that memory sitting in front of you.

- ❑ Imagine sending them compassion and kindness. Speak to them as you would a close friend—what would you say to reassure them and help them heal?

- ❑ After the meditation, reflect on how this exercise impacted your perception of yourself and your emotions.

_____

_____

_____

_____

Activity 2: Burn a Letter Ritual

- ❑ Write a letter detailing your feelings of guilt, shame, or resentment. Pour your emotions into the letter, articulating how these feelings have affected your life.

- ❑ Once completed, find a safe space outdoors or in a well-ventilated area.

- ❑ With mindfulness, read the letter aloud one final time, then safely burn it, visualizing the release of those burdens with the flames.

- ❑ Reflect on the experience: How does it feel to have let go of those emotions? What did you learn about your healing process?

_____

_____

_____

_____

Activity 3: Mindful Breathing Exercise

- ❑ Set aside 5–10 minutes in a quiet space.

- ❑ Begin with deep, rhythmic breaths: inhale for a count of four, hold for a count of one, and exhale for a count of five.

- ❑ Focus on the sensations in your body as you breathe, noticing any tension or discomfort tied to your emotions.

- ❑ Reflect on how this mindfulness exercise helps detach from guilt, shame, or resentment, allowing you to return to the present moment with greater clarity.

_____

_____

_____

Activity 4: Body Scan Meditation

- ❑ Lie down comfortably in a quiet environment.

- ❑ Close your eyes and take several deep breaths, allowing your body to relax.

- ❑ Slowly focus your attention on each part of your body, starting from your toes and moving to the top of your head.

- ❑ Acknowledge any sensations you feel—tension, discomfort, or softness—and breathe into those areas to facilitate release.

- ❑ Write about the insights gained from this practice and how it helps you connect emotions to physical sensations.

_____

_____

_____

_____

Engaging Alternative Practices

Activity 1: Physical Release Techniques

- ❏ Choose an activity that allows you to physically express your emotions. This could involve shaking out your body, dancing, or engaging in a form of exercise that feels freeing.
- ❏ After the activity, take a few moments to journal about your experience, noting any emotions you released or any clarity you gained about your childhood experiences

_____

_____

Activity 2: Art Therapy Exploration

- ❏ Create an art piece that represents a painful memory or feeling. Use colors, shapes, or materials that resonate with your emotions.
- ❏ Reflect on the process afterward. What did creating the piece reveal about your feelings regarding that memory? Did you uncover new insights or release emotions through your art?

_____

_____

Journaling for Clarity and Accountability

Activity 1: Let-It-Go Journal

- ❏ Keep a journal for one week where you document instances of guilt, shame, or resentment as they arise.
- ❏ For each entry, note the context, your emotional reaction, and any underlying triggers (thoughts, situations, or people involved).
- ❏ Write affirmations that you are letting these feelings go, and setting yourself free

_____

_____

_____

Activity 2: Celebrating Small Victories

- ❑ Dedicate a page in your journal to celebrate small victories in your journey toward letting go of negative emotions.

- ❑ Write down at least three moments from the past week when you successfully managed guilt, shame, or resentment.

- ❑ Reflect on how each victory makes you feel and how it reinforces your commitment to emotional healing.

_____

_____

_____

Building Your Support System

Activity 1: Identifying Supportive Friends and Family

- ❑ Create a list of people in your life who uplift and encourage you.

- ❑ Next to each name, note specific qualities or actions that make them supportive.

- ❑ Consider reaching out to these individuals for support as you navigate your emotional journey. What specific conversation or topic would you like to discuss with them?

_____

_____

_____

_____

Activity 2: Establishing an Accountability Partnership

- ❑ Choose a trusted friend or family member to be your accountability partner in your journey of releasing guilt, shame, and resentment.

- ❑ Plan a regular check-in schedule (weekly or bi-weekly) where you can discuss your progress and any challenges you face.

❑ Commit to sharing your feelings during these meetings and encouraging each other's growth through supportive dialogue.

___

Looking Ahead

As you work through these exercises, notice how your relationship with guilt, shame, and resentment evolves. In the next chapter, we'll explore understanding and overcoming self-sabotaging behaviors.

Final Reflection

What's your key takeaway from this chapter?

___

What practice will you start with tomorrow?

___

Your Personal Notes

Use this space for additional thoughts and insights:

___

CHAPTER 3:

Understanding and Overcoming Self-Sabotaging Behaviors

Understanding and overcoming self-sabotaging behaviors is a journey that invites your introspection and growth. These behaviors often emerge from hidden patterns within yourself, triggered by stress, fear, or past experiences. They can manifest in various forms, such as procrastination, negative self-talk, or perfectionism, causing you to hinder your progress unconsciously.

In this chapter, we'll discover how awareness helps to change self-sabotaging habits into more constructive ones.

Quick Check-In Exercise

Before we explore self-sabotaging behaviors, take a moment to check in with yourself:

Rate your current level (1–10):

❑ Awareness of self-sabotaging patterns: _____

❑ Readiness to explore change: _____

❑ Self-compassion when facing challenges: _____

What behaviors do you suspect might be self-sabotaging?

_____

When do these behaviors typically appear?

_____

What would success in changing these patterns look like?

Essential Steps to Counteract Self-Sabotage

This section guides you through the essential steps to identify and counteract self-sabotaging behaviors. It explores the significance of recognizing triggers and replacing self-destructive habits with healthier alternatives. Beginning with the roots of these behaviors, you will learn to develop proactive strategies for managing your reactions to stressors and fears.

Regular Introspection

Mindfulness, regular introspection, and conscious decision-making are useful tools for fostering self-awareness. It's also important to emphasize the empowerment that comes from active decision-making and setting realistic goals tailored to your circumstances.

Crafting an Effective Action Plan

You will discover how an effective action plan and external support systems can aid in overcoming these challenges. Through reflection and accountability, this chapter offers a road map for transforming harmful habits and embracing resilience, leading to long-lasting change and personal fulfillment.

Understanding Triggers

Recognizing and overcoming self-sabotaging behaviors involves taking a deep look into what sets off these detrimental actions and cultivating strategies for their replacement. Understanding triggers is vital in this process, as they are specific events, thoughts, or emotions that prompt a self-sabotaging response.

Self-Awareness and Behavioral Patterns

Self-awareness is foundational in recognizing patterns of behavior that lead to self-sabotage. Regular introspection and mindfulness can aid in visibility, allowing you to catch yourself in moments where you habitually resort to self-sabotage.

Identifying Common Self-Destructive Habits

Understanding common self-destructive habits is essential because it provides insight into broader behavioral patterns and offers reassurance that these struggles are not unique to you.

The Role of Active Decision-Making

Active decision-making plays a critical role in replacing harmful behaviors with positive ones. When you take ownership of your choices, you empower yourself to make deliberate decisions rather than defaulting to automatic, potentially damaging reactions.

Goalsetting In Your Action Plan

Building on self-awareness and decision-making, crafting a tailored action plan with goal-setting significantly enhances your commitment and accountability. Setting clear, attainable objectives enables you to measure progress and adapt strategies as needed.

Importance of Self-Reflection

An effective action plan includes regular self-reflection to evaluate your progress and adjust tactics accordingly. Over time, this reflective practice can illuminate aspects of your mindset that previously went unnoticed.

Interactive Exercise: Pattern Recognition Map

Take a moment to map out your self-sabotaging patterns:

Situation Analysis

- ❑ Common triggering situations: _____
- ❑ Emotions that arise: _____
- ❑ Typical reactions: _____
- ❑ Impact on my goals: _____

Pattern Timeline

- ❑ Morning triggers: _____
- ❑ Afternoon challenges: _____
- ❑ Evening patterns: _____
- ❑ Weekend variations: _____

Response Inventory

- ❑ Current coping methods: _____
- ❑ What works: _____
- ❑ What doesn't work: _____
- ❑ New strategies to try: _____

Support System Check

- ❑ Who helps me stay accountable: _____
- ❑ Resources I can access: _____
- ❑ Tools I find helpful: _____
- ❑ Additional support needed: _____

Choose one pattern to focus on this week:

- ❑ Pattern I'll work with: _____
- ❑ Small step to take: _____
- ❑ How I'll track progress: _____

The Role of External Support

Accountability plays a vital role in your journey of overcoming self-sabotaging behaviors. Engaging others in your goal-setting process provides external motivation that can be invaluable during challenging periods.

Establishing Accountability Partnerships

Establishing connections with accountability partners is crucial for accountability success. Choosing a supportive partner who understands your aspirations can reinforce your efforts and maintain your commitment. Regular check-in meetings with your accountability partner create an opportunity to discuss progress, address setbacks, and recalibrate efforts as necessary.

Journaling as an Accountability Tool

Journaling serves as a highly effective personal tool for maintaining your accountability. It encourages you to observe behavior patterns, identify self-sabotage triggers, and evaluate how your responses contribute to achieving your goals.

Monitoring your progress is equally important and should be incorporated into your accountability framework. Acknowledge and celebrate your small victories along the way to reinforce positive behavior. Use your journal to help you track your progress.

More Practical Exercises

Explore a variety of engaging exercises designed to reconnect with and nurture your inner child throughout this workbook.

Formulating a Self-Sabotage Breakthrough Plan

To effectively address self-sabotaging behaviors, create a structured plan.

Identify 3 Self-Sabotaging Behaviors

Reflect on specific instances where you have engaged in self-sabotage. This could be procrastination, excessive self-criticism, or avoiding opportunities. Write down these behaviors.

_____

_____

_____

Write a Plan for Interrupting Each Behavior

For each identified behavior, note strategies to interrupt these patterns. This could involve setting reminders, enlisting an accountability partner, or developing alternative responses.

_____

_____

_____

_____

Track Your Progress Over 7 Days

Keep a daily log for one week to monitor your attempts to interrupt these behaviors. Observe the situations, your feelings, and how you responded.

_____

_____

_____

_____

Visual Progress Tracker

- ❑ Create a visual progress tracker (like a chart or journal layout) that outlines your goals related to overcoming self-sabotage.

- ❑ Include specific milestones along the journey, such as reframing negative thoughts or seeking support.

- ❑ Regularly update this tracker and celebrate small victories by noting them down, reflecting on how each step brings you closer to your goals.

_____

_____

_____

_____

Letter-Writing Exercises

Heartfelt Letter to Your Inner Child

Write a heartfelt letter to your inner child, acknowledging moments when you felt scared or unsupported.

Reflect on how these feelings may have contributed to your self-sabotaging behaviors.

Offer words of compassion and encouragement, reminding your inner child that it's okay to make mistakes and that you are committed to nurturing and protecting them moving forward.

Express your intention to create a safe space for growth and healing, outlining the steps you'll take to support them better.

_____

_____

_____

_____

Letter to Your Caregivers

Compose a letter to your caregivers (past or present) expressing the emotions tied to their actions during your childhood.

- ❏ Be honest about how their behaviors may have impacted your self-esteem and contributed to your self-sabotaging patterns.

- ❏ While writing, consider any unresolved feelings you wish to address and seek closure or understanding.

- ❏ After writing, reflect on what you learned about yourself in terms of forgiveness and moving forward.

_____

_____

_____

_____

Guided Reframing of Painful Memories and Limiting Beliefs

Activity: Reframing Negative Memories

- ❑ Choose a painful memory that triggers self-sabotaging behaviors. In your journal, describe the memory in detail, including your emotions and thoughts at the time.

- ❑ Next, write a reframed version of this memory. Imagine how you would like to see yourself respond differently, with compassion and strength.

- ❑ What positive outcomes could arise from this new perspective? How does reframing this memory alter the way you feel about yourself and your current challenges?

_____

_____

_____

_____

Activity: Unpacking Limiting Beliefs

- ❑ Identify a limiting belief that contributes to your self-sabotage (like "I'm not good enough" or "I always fail"). Write it down in your journal.

- ❑ Explore the origin of this belief: When did you first adopt it, and how has it impacted your actions?

- ❑ Reframe this belief by writing a supportive and empowering statement that counters the limiting belief. Repeat this new belief daily, noting any shifts in your mindset and habits.

_____

_____

_____

_____

Creative Activities to Release Negative Emotions

Activity: Creative Therapy Exercise

- ❏ Gather art supplies (colored pencils, paints, or clay) and create a visual representation of your self-sabotaging behavior.
- ❏ As you create, allow your feelings about this behavior to guide your artistic expression—be it through colors, shapes, or textures.
- ❏ After completing your artwork, write a brief reflection on how the process felt and what emotions were released. Consider how this creative exploration can serve as a tool for healing.

_____

_____

_____

Looking Ahead

As you work through these exercises, notice how your awareness of self-sabotaging patterns evolves. In the next chapter, we'll explore how to rewrite the limiting beliefs rooted in childhood.

Final Reflection

What's your key takeaway from this chapter?

_____

What practice will you start with tomorrow?

_____

Your Personal Notes

Use this space for additional thoughts and insights:

_____

_____

CHAPTER 4:

Rewriting Limiting Beliefs Rooted in Childhood

Rewriting limiting beliefs rooted in childhood is a journey that opens the door to personal growth and emotional healing. These early-formed beliefs often shape how we perceive ourselves and the world, sometimes as barriers to our adult potential. Seeking transformation, understanding, and reshaping these beliefs can be pivotal in achieving a more fulfilling life. This process involves facing deeply ingrained perceptions and turning them into opportunities for self-discovery and empowerment. It's about recognizing that what once seemed like unchangeable truths can be rewritten into narratives of strength and confidence.

In this chapter, we'll explore practical techniques to reframe childhood beliefs, focusing on the power of affirmations to reinforce positive mindsets.

Quick Check-In Exercise

Before we explore limiting beliefs, take a moment to check in with yourself:

_____

_____

Rate your current level (1–10):

- ❑ Awareness of limiting beliefs: _____

- ❑ Openness to new perspectives: _____

- ❑ Self-trust: _____

What beliefs do you suspect might be holding you back?

_____

_____

Where did you first learn these beliefs?

_____

_____

What new beliefs would you like to develop?

_____

_____

Use Affirmations to Reinforce Positive Beliefs

Affirmations can be powerful tools to reshape limiting beliefs formed in childhood, transforming them into positive statements that promote self-acceptance and growth. Understanding affirmations is crucial for you if you seek to change your perception of self-worth. At their core, affirmations are positive statements or phrases you repeat to challenge negative thoughts. They work by helping you reframe your inner dialogue from one of self-doubt to one of confidence and positivity. For instance, instead of dwelling on a belief like "I am not good enough," you might say, "I am worthy and capable." These statements lay the groundwork for a more positive self-image and bolster your self-worth over time.

Tailor Affirmations to Reparent Your Inner Child

Writing personal affirmations is an intentional process that involves crafting statements tailored to resonate with your experiences and goals. Personalization is key, ensuring that the affirmations speak directly to your unique circumstances and emotional needs. Effective affirmations should be clear, specific, and reflect the desired state of mind or behavior. For example, affirming "I take action and complete my tasks with ease" can be empowering if you struggle with procrastination. Regularly revisiting these affirmations is essential, allowing you to refine and adapt them as you grow, deepening their impact and effectiveness.

Incorporating Affirmations Into Daily Life

Integrating affirmations into your daily life involves incorporating them seamlessly into your routine. You can do this by repeating affirmations during your morning rituals or engaging in activities like journaling or meditation. The power of repetition cannot be understated; consistent practice helps reinforce the messages and gradually shifts your thought patterns toward more constructive outcomes. Documenting affirmations can also help you track progress and encourage accountability. Writing them down in a visible place, such as a journal or on sticky notes around your house, is a constant reminder to focus on positive self-talk and embrace change.

Overcoming Limiting Beliefs

Fighting limiting beliefs with affirmations requires understanding specific beliefs that need reframing. The first step is to identify these beliefs, which involves introspection and honest self-assessment to recognize which thoughts hold you back. Once identified, response strategies can be developed, such as turning the belief "I will never succeed" into an affirmation like "I am open to new opportunities and capable of achieving success."

Transforming a negative belief into a positive assertion is powerful; it marks a shift from a fixed mindset to a growth-oriented one. Celebrating even small progress along the journey reinforces the effectiveness of affirmations and helps maintain motivation; recognizing achievements, no matter how minor, builds momentum and fosters a sense of accomplishment.

Long-Term Changes Through Consistent Practice

Consistently practicing affirmations can lead to long-term changes in beliefs. As one continues to engage with affirmations, it becomes easier to internalize these positive messages, thereby naturally reducing the prevalence of limiting beliefs. Studies suggest that when practiced consistently, affirmations can enhance well-being, boost self-esteem, and foster a resilient mindset ready to tackle life's challenges (Critcher & Dunning, 2015).

Incorporating affirmations into therapy or coaching sessions can provide structure and support, offering clients a practical tool for emotional healing and personal transformation. For mental health professionals, guiding clients through the creation and application of tailored affirmations can enrich the therapeutic process, enabling clients to reclaim agency over their narratives and achieve their personal growth goals.

Interactive Exercise: Belief Transformation Map

Take a moment to map your beliefs and their potential transformations:

Current Belief System

What I believe about myself:

___

Where this belief came from:

___

How it affects my choices:

___

What it protects me from:

___

Evidence Collection

Times this belief wasn't true:

___

Successes that challenge it:

___

People who see me differently:

___

New experiences that disprove it:

___

New Belief Creation

What I choose to believe now:

___

Evidence supporting this new belief:

_____

How it will serve me better:

_____

First step toward embodying it:

_____

Support for Change

People who can help:

_____

Resources I can use:

_____

Daily practices to reinforce:

_____

How I'll celebrate progress:

_____

Visualize Desired Outcomes to Instill New Beliefs

Visualization is a powerful mental practice that bridges the gap between our current state and our emotional aspirations. By harnessing the brain's ability to rehearse experiences mentally, visualization allows individuals to manifest their goals and reshape their beliefs. This practice is rooted in the principle that thought precedes action, paving the way for success by mentally mapping out desired outcomes before they occur.

At its core, visualization leverages neuroplasticity—the brain's capacity to form new neural pathways. When we consistently visualize positive outcomes, these pathways strengthen, reinforcing the mindset necessary for achieving our goals. Visualization isn't confined to mental imagery; it involves engaging all five senses to create a rich, immersive experience that trickles into our everyday reality. Vividly imagining a scenario activates parts of the brain associated with real-life execution, thus preparing an individual for actual performance (Toronto, 2022).

Techniques for Effective Visualization

To fully harness visualization's benefits, employing techniques that enhance its effectiveness is essential. The first step is to create a conducive environment. Select a quiet space with limited interruptions. This setting should be comfortable, allowing you to relax and focus solely on the visualization practice. Once settled, close your eyes and take deep breaths to enter a state of calmness.

Develop detailed mental images by using abundant specificity. Imagine the visual aspects of success and how it feels, sounds, smells, and tastes. Engaging multiple senses imbues the visualization with a lifelike quality, making it more effective. For instance, if you're visualizing delivering a successful presentation, immerse yourself in the sound of applause, feel the smoothness of the podium, and see the smiles on your audience's faces.

It's also beneficial to seamlessly incorporate visualization practices into daily routines. Incorporating morning visualizations can set a positive tone for the day, while visualizing before bedtime reinforces hopes and dreams as you drift off to sleep. Regular and deliberate practice ultimately strengthens the connection between mental imagery and tangible outcomes.

Combining Visualization with Affirmations

Visualization gains an exponential impact when combined with affirmations. These statements act as positive reinforcements, anchoring the visualized scenarios to belief systems that promote change. To integrate both practices effectively, synchronize your visual images with relevant affirmations. For example, as you envision overcoming a challenge, affirm aloud, "I am capable of navigating this with confidence."

Affirmations should be simple, specific, and resonate with personal truths. Writing them down enhances commitment, serving as reminders throughout the day, which amplifies their effect. Integrating affirmations into morning routines creates a routine anchored in positivity and self-belief, setting the stage for a proactive approach to challenges. This combination gradually shifts mindsets, embedding new truths that counteract limiting beliefs.

Applying Visualization to Overcome Obstacles

Visualization is instrumental in reframing narratives around personal limitations and boosting confidence in overcoming obstacles. Begin by identifying specific challenges rooted in childhood beliefs. Then, create vivid mental images of successfully navigating these obstacles. This rehearsal builds a subconscious blueprint for real-time execution, fostering a sense of preparedness and empowerment.

Consider someone who developed a fear of public speaking during school. They might visualize themselves standing confidently before an audience, speaking fluidly, and receiving enthusiastic applause. By replaying this scenario repeatedly, the individual rewires their perception of public speaking, shifting from fear to confidence. Visualization thus acts as a catalyst for dismantling restrictive beliefs and promoting resilience and adaptability.

Applying visualization helps transform perceived weaknesses into strengths, encouraging a new narrative built on perseverance and achievement. The practice invites individuals to reimagine their potential, bolstering a journey toward personal growth and emotional healing.

More Practical Exercises

Explore engaging exercises designed to reconnect with and nurture your inner child throughout this workbook.

Crafting Unique Affirmations

Activity 1: Identifying Limiting Beliefs

- ❏ Identify at least three limiting beliefs that you hold about yourself. Examples may include "I am not worthy" or "I will never succeed."

_____

_____

_____

Activity 2: Creating Empowering Affirmations

- ❏ Transform each limiting belief into a positive affirmation. For example, change "I am not worthy" to "I am deserving of love and success."

❑ Write these affirmations in your journal, ensuring they resonate with your true self and aspirations. Make them clear, specific, and focused on the qualities you wish to cultivate.

❑ Commit to practicing your affirmations daily. Please choose a time (morning or evening) to recite them aloud.

Visualization Techniques for Empowerment

Activity 1: Vision of Success

❑ Identify a goal or challenge you wish to overcome rooted in a limiting belief.

❑ Take a quiet moment to visualize yourself successfully achieving this goal. Use all your senses to create a vivid mental picture. What do you see, hear, and feel as you succeed?

❑ Write about this visualization experience in your journal, detailing the emotions and sensations you encountered.

Activity 2: Affirmation during Visualization

❑ Pair your visualization with the affirmations you crafted. As you imagine overcoming your challenge, repeat the relevant affirmations.

❑ Write about how combining these practices enhances the effectiveness of your visualization.

Self-Reflection and Growth Tracking

Activity 1: Progress Journal

- ❏ Maintain a progress journal to track your emotional and behavioral shifts as you work on rewriting your limiting beliefs.

_____

_____

Activity 2: Celebrating Your Achievements

- ❏ At the end of each month, recognize and celebrate your progress. List at least three accomplishments related to overcoming limiting beliefs, no matter how small.

_____

_____

_____

Looking Ahead

As you work through these exercises, notice how your relationship with your beliefs evolves. In the next chapter, we'll investigate how to build emotional freedom and peace.

Final Reflection

What's your key takeaway from this chapter?

_____

_____

What practice will you start with tomorrow?

_____

_____

_____

Your Personal Notes

Use this space for additional thoughts and insights:

CHAPTER 5:

Building Emotional Freedom and Peace

Building emotional freedom and peace involves understanding and nurturing one's inner landscape, creating a sense of balance that extends to all areas of life. While many external factors can disrupt this equilibrium, cultivating self-awareness and resilience allows individuals to navigate these challenges with greater ease. The quest for emotional freedom is not about avoiding life's hardships or emotions but rather developing the capacity to face them without feeling overwhelmed. Through intentional practices and thoughtful reflection, you are invited to begin a journey toward lasting peace and fulfillment.

This chapter explores various strategies designed to empower you in your pursuit for emotional well-being.

Quick Check-In Exercise

Before we explore building emotional freedom, take a moment to check in with yourself:

Rate your current level (1–10):

- ❏ Emotional freedom: _____
- ❏ Inner peace: _____
- ❏ Connection with self: _____

What makes you feel most free emotionally?

_____

What brings you peace right now?

_____

_____

What support do you need on this journey?

_____

_____

Establish Your Daily Mindfulness Practice

Incorporating mindfulness into daily life is a powerful strategy for emotional well-being. It offers a gateway to understanding our mental states, managing stress, and enhancing resilience. Mindfulness Meditation, an essential component of this practice, helps anchor our attention in the present. This form of meditation reduces anxiety and stress by allowing individuals to let go of past regrets and future worries. Instead, it promotes self-awareness and resilience by encouraging us to engage fully with the present moment. By focusing on current experiences without judgment, mindfulness enables us to respond to situations thoughtfully rather than react impulsively (Mayo Clinic Staff, 2022).

Starting Small With Mindfulness Meditation

For many, mindfulness meditation starts small—with just a few minutes a day—progressing as you become more comfortable with the practice. This form of exercise is not restricted to seated meditation. Techniques like mindful breathing can be seamlessly integrated into various daily activities. The simple act of focusing on your breath, observing each inhale and exhale, serves as an immediate source of relief from distress. Breath awareness techniques regulate your emotions by slowing down racing thoughts, thereby promoting calmness. These exercises are accessible anywhere—from waiting in line to sitting at your desk—making them easy to incorporate into your routine.

Enhancing Emotional Stability With Gratitude Journaling

Gratitude journaling offers another avenue to enhance your emotional stability. This practice involves documenting positive experiences or aspects of your life regularly. It helps shift your focus away from negativity and fosters a more balanced mood by retraining your mind to see positivity even during tough times. Re-reading these entries can serve as a reminder of the good that exists, acting as a buffer against life's inevitable challenges. Regular gratitude journaling builds a habit of seeking joy, which in turn contributes to your long-term emotional health.

Combining Physical Activity With Mindfulness

Mindful movement combines physical activity with the principles of mindfulness. Practices such as yoga or tai chi integrate gentle movements with breath control and meditation, improving both your physical health and emotional clarity. These activities reduce feelings of overwhelm by encouraging balance between your body and mind. They promote a deeper connection with your physical state, enhancing awareness of bodily sensations and emotional responses. The regular pursuit of mindful movement leads to improved posture, flexibility, and strength, simultaneously supporting your mental peace and relaxation.

Embracing Mindfulness for Emotional Freedom

You unlock the potential for emotional freedom and peace as you embrace mindfulness in its many forms—whether through structured meditation, breath awareness, gratitude journaling, or mindful movement. This holistic approach equips you with tools to navigate life's complexities with grace and resilience. You are empowered to break free from cycles of stress and anxiety, opening up new possibilities for personal growth and transformation.

Commitment to Mindfulness Strategies

Implementing these strategies requires commitment but offers considerable rewards. As you begin your journey into mindfulness, it may be helpful to set aside a dedicated time each day for practice, gradually increasing duration as your comfort levels rise. Consistency is key; over time, what once felt awkward or difficult becomes a natural part of your routine. The ultimate goal is not perfection but progress—cultivating a mindset of patience and compassion toward yourself.

Transforming Lives Through Mindfulness

Mindfulness practices can transform not only your life but also ripple outwards to benefit others. As you become more attuned to your inner world, you may find yourself better equipped to engage empathetically with those around you. The enhanced emotional regulation and reduced reactivity fostered by mindfulness create an environment conducive to healthier relationships and a more harmonious community.

Integrating Mindfulness in Professional Settings

For mental health professionals and coaches seeking to integrate mindfulness into their practices, these methods offer a wealth of opportunities to support clients' emotional healing. Guiding you through mindful exercises can provide invaluable insights into their emotional triggers and coping mechanisms. Tailoring mindfulness techniques to suit each client's unique needs enriches your clients' growth processes and facilitates lasting change.

Interactive Exercise: Freedom and Peace Mapping

Take a moment to map your journey toward emotional freedom:

Peace Anchors

- ❑ Places I feel peaceful: _____
- ❑ Activities that bring calm: _____
- ❑ People who support peace: _____
- ❑ Practices that ground me: _____

Freedom Inventory

- ❑ When I feel most free: _____
- ❑ What liberation feels like: _____
- ❑ What holds me back: _____
- ❑ Steps toward freedom: _____

Daily Practice Design

- ❑ Morning peace ritual: _____
- ❑ Midday check-in: _____

❑ Evening wind-down: _____

❑ Weekend recharge: _____

Personal Sanctuary Creation

❑ Physical space needs: _____

❑ Emotional environment: _____

❑ Boundaries to maintain: _____

❑ Support to gather: _____

Choose one area to focus on this week:

❑ Focus area: _____

❑ First small step: _____

❑ How I'll track progress: _____

Practicing Self-Care

An essential component supporting your wellness is practicing self-care. Prioritizing your emotional needs is critical because it provides the energy and clarity needed to enforce boundaries consistently. Self-care means different things to different people; for some, it could involve regular exercise, while others might benefit from mindfulness practices or spending time in nature. For each self-care strategy, write one or two practical ways you will implement it this week.

Regular Exercise

❑ **Suggestions:** Create a weekly exercise routine that includes activities you enjoy, such as yoga, dancing, hiking, or swimming. Aim for at least 30 minutes of movement most days of the week.

❑ **Example:** If you love being outdoors, schedule a nature walk or hike every weekend. Join a local fitness class or start with home workout videos.

Self-Compassion Rituals

- **Suggestions:** Create a self-compassion ritual that allows you to acknowledge your feelings without judgment. This may involve affirmations, guided visualizations, or simple self-reflection.

- **Example:** Each night before bed, look in the mirror and recite three affirmations that resonate with you, such as "I am enough," "I deserve happiness," and "I am learning and growing every day."

___
___

Quality Time in Nature

- **Suggestions:** Spend time outdoors regularly to recharge and gain perspective. Nature has a calming effect that can help soothe emotional disturbances.

- **Example:** Plan a weekly outing to a nearby park, beach, or nature reserve, allowing yourself to explore, relax, and practice mindfulness among the trees and water.

___
___

Creative Expression

- **Suggestions:** Engage in creative hobbies that allow self-expression, such as painting, writing, music, or crafting. These activities can serve as an outlet for exploring emotions and reduce stress.

- **Example:** Start a weekly art evening where you dedicate an hour to drawing or painting, regardless of your skill level. You can also journal creatively through poetry or storytelling.

___
___

Social Connections

- ❑ **Suggestions:** Nurture relationships with supportive friends or family members by scheduling regular catch-ups and open dialogues about your feelings and experiences.

- ❑ **Example:** Establish a monthly "self-care day" with a friend to engage in enjoyable activities together—this could be going for coffee, taking a class, or having a movie night.

_____

_____

Healthy Nutrition

- ❑ **Suggestions:** Focus on nourishing your body with wholesome foods. Meal planning can simplify the process and ensure you're fueling your body with nutrient-rich options.

- ❑ **Example:** Dedicate a few hours each week to meal prep, creating healthy meals that you can easily access during busy days. Experiment with new recipes that excite your palate and contribute to your well-being.

_____

_____

_____

Unplugging from Technology

- ❑ **Suggestions:** Designate tech-free zones or times to create mental space. Consistent breaks from screens can enhance your mood and allow for more mindful interactions.

- ❑ **Example:** Establish a "no phone" policy during meals or before bedtime, encouraging deeper conversations and better sleep hygiene.

_____

_____

_____

Treating your needs with respect and incorporating self-care practices into your daily life, you create a nurturing environment for yourself. Consequently, it becomes easier for others to follow suit, leading to more fulfilling and balanced relationships.

More Practical Exercises

Explore a variety of engaging exercises designed to reconnect with and nurture your inner child throughout this workbook.

Mindfulness Practices for Emotional Release

Activity 1: Intentional Breathing Exercise

- ❑ Find a quiet space where you can sit comfortably. Close your eyes and take a deep breath in for a count of four, hold for a count of four, and exhale slowly for a count of six.

- ❑ Repeat this practice for five minutes, focusing solely on your breath. When your mind wanders, gently bring your attention back to your breathing.

- ❑ After the exercise, journal about your experience. What thoughts or feelings arose during the practice?

_____

_____

_____

Activity 2: Gratitude Journaling

- ❑ Spend a few minutes each day for a week writing down three things you are grateful for. These can be small or significant.

- ❑ At the end of the week, reflect on how focusing on gratitude affected your mood and perspective.

_____

_____

_____

Establishing and Communicating Personal Boundaries

Activity 1: Identifying Your Boundaries

- ❑ Create a list of personal boundaries that you feel are necessary to maintain your emotional health. Consider areas such as time, energy, and emotional investment in relationships.

- ❑ For each boundary, write down specific situations where you feel this boundary might be important.

_____

_____

_____

Activity 2: Communicating Your Boundaries

- ❑ Choose one boundary from your list to practice communicating. Write down how you would express this boundary clearly and assertively, using "I" statements.

- ❑ Role-play or rehearse this communication with a trusted friend or in front of a mirror.

_____

_____

_____

Building Your Support System

Activity 1: Identifying Supportive Relationships

- ❑ List the people in your life who provide emotional support and contribute positively to your well-being.

- ❑ Consider ways to deepen these connections by planning a casual meet-up or a shared activity.

_____

_____

Activity 2: Establishing Accountability Partnerships

❑ Choose a friend or family member to be your accountability partner as you work on building emotional freedom. Write down the goals and the strategies you wish to implement from this chapter.

❑ Schedule regular check-ins to discuss your progress, challenges, and successes.

_____

_____

_____

Looking Ahead

As you conclude this workbook, notice how your journey toward emotional freedom and peace continues to evolve. Remember that healing is ongoing, and each step forward is progress.

Final Reflection

What's your key takeaway from this chapter?

_____

_____

What practice will you start with tomorrow?

_____

_____

Your Personal Notes

Use this space for additional thoughts and insights:

_____

_____

_____

CONCLUSION

In concluding our journey, we have explored emotional healing and personal transformation, uncovering the layered complexities that define who we are. Understanding emotional patterns is like assembling puzzle pieces from our past, particularly from our formative years. These patterns are not mere relics; they actively shape our current perceptions and reactions. When we recognize these themes, we gain insights into our triggers and automatic behaviors, paving the way for healthier relationships and thoughtful responses.

Can you imagine the empowerment of recognizing these patterns? It's like lifting a veil obscuring self-awareness. This insight enables us to face challenges with intention rather than reflexive reactions, allowing for the transformation of outdated behaviors into present-day interactions. This evolution revitalizes our connections through understanding and respect.

Forgiveness plays an enormous role in this journey. Although it is often misunderstood, it is a liberating force. Forgiveness does not erase the past but frees us from the burdens of resentment and guilt, redirecting our emotional energy toward growth and healing. By forgiving, we clear the space for emotional liberation, enhancing our purpose and peace.

Confronting self-sabotage is vital. These behaviors often manifest as procrastination or avoidance, arising from fear or uncertainty. Identifying and replacing these patterns allows us to cultivate resilience and pursue our aspirations with confidence. Establishing personal boundaries is equally essential, as they safeguard our mental health and encourage meaningful interactions. Boundaries nurture authentic relationships and remind us that prioritizing our well-being is vital for a balanced life.

As we continue this unique journey of growth and transformation, may this be a guide toward authenticity, resilience, and fulfillment. Embrace the richness of your experiences, knowing each contributes to your evolution. Remember, emotional healing is a shared human experience, and with each step, you inspire healing and profound change. Let this journey illuminate your path forward, filled with hope and possibility.

If you've enjoyed this workbook, join us again in *Workbook 4: Inner Child Relationships: Break Negative Patterns, Improve Communication, and Build Authentic Connections* to continue this journey.

BOOK 4

Inner Child Relationships

Negative Patterns, Improve Communication, and Build Authentic Connections

INTRODUCTION

In the quiet recesses of our minds lies a child whose voice whispers faintly, often unheard. This inner child holds onto dreams, fears, and experiences that shape us and influence our relationships. Navigating adult relationships can feel like an intricate dance, colored by echoes of the past. Emotional barriers from childhood can become walls, hindering genuine connections and leaving us yearning for intimacy.

This book serves as a guiding light on the journey of healing, encouraging readers to face their inner child and listen to its stories. Engaging with this workbook is a choice to step onto a life-changing path where unresolved childhood wounds no longer dictate interactions. The exercises and insights aim to break longstanding patterns, inviting healthier, more authentic connections.

Statistics show nearly 70% of adults carry childhood scars that shape relationships (Springer et al., 2003). These figures highlight a shared human experience, illustrating how early life events resonate through our connections. Understanding vulnerabilities with curiosity rather than fear enables us to recognize stories lying beneath defensive behaviors.

Common relationship dynamics may repeat due to childhood attachment styles formed by our bonds with caregivers. Understanding these styles helps peel away defenses and reveals insights into our relational behaviors.

Key chapters guide the process of building relationships:

1) **The Link Between Childhood Trauma and Relationship Patterns**
2) **Recognizing and Breaking Free from Toxic Dynamics**
3) **Trusting and Communicating Effectively**
4) **Fostering Emotional Vulnerability and Authentic Connections**
5) **Building Strong, Healthy Relationships**

Take the chance to escape from patterns that trap you and create new paths for healing and happiness. This journey is hard but brings great rewards: trusting relationships, better self-awareness, and more joy. Healing isn't a straight line; every small step helps you rediscover your true self and grow.

Let this be the moment you choose to rewrite past stories, developing connections that reflect your true essence. Welcome to a journey where transformation awaits—not just in your relationships, but within yourself.

CHAPTER 1:

The Link Between Childhood Trauma and Relationship Patterns

Understanding how childhood trauma affects adult relationships is critical for personal growth. Early experiences shape how you connect with others later in life.

This chapter helps you reflect on your past, you can uncover behaviors rooted in trauma, leading to greater self-awareness and healing.

Recognizing Trauma-Triggered Behavioral Patterns

Childhood trauma influences adult relational dynamics. Triggers—seemingly innocuous events that provoke strong emotional responses—often stem from past experiences. Recognizing these triggers allows you to manage emotional responses effectively and foster healthier interactions.

Identifying Common Self-Destructive Behaviors

Common behaviors linked to childhood trauma include:

- ❏ **Avoidance:** Staying away from close relationships due to fear of abandonment.
- ❏ **Clinginess:** Seeking excessive reassurance from partners due to past instability.
- ❏ **Distrust:** Questioning others' intentions based on previous betrayals.
- ❏ **Heightened sensitivity:** Reacting intensely to criticism linked to childhood ridicule.

Relationship Mapping Exercise

To deepen your understanding of relationship patterns, engage in a relationship mapping exercise:

1) Create two columns: Draw two columns labeled Positive Relationships and Negative Relationships.

2) List relationships: In each column, list your past and present relationships (family, friends, romantic).

3) Identify patterns: For each relationship, answer these questions in the space provided below:

   a) What attachment style do you exhibit (secure, anxious, avoidant)?

   b) How do you typically react during conflicts?

   c) Are there recurring themes or behaviors (e.g., fear of abandonment, withdrawal)?

   d) What emotions do you feel during vulnerable moments?

_____

_____

_____

This exercise will help you identify patterns shaped by childhood experiences, leading to insights into your current relational dynamics.

Becoming Aware of Existing Relationship Patterns

Awareness as Your First Step

Notice behaviors such as:

- ❏ avoidance
- ❏ clinginess
- ❏ distrust
- ❏ emotional sensitivity
- ❏ reflect on your past experiences.

Actionable Steps

_____

_____

_____

Journaling

Use journaling to visualize your feelings.

- ❏ Recognize patterns over time.
- ❏ Write to reveal connections between past experiences and current behaviors.
- ❏ Set aside a few minutes daily for reflection to enhance self-understanding.

Actionable Steps

_____

_____

_____

Identifying Root Causes

Seek therapy or counseling for deeper emotional issues.

- ❏ **Therapeutic support:**
  - A licensed therapist can provide:
    - ➢ Tools and strategies for managing trauma-related behaviors.
    - ➢ Guidance in developing healthier relationships.
    - ➢ Support while working through painful memories.
- ❏ **Engaging in trauma-informed therapy:**
  - Rebuild your sense of safety within relationships.
  - Learn new coping mechanisms.

Actionable Steps

_____

_____

_____

Empowerment

Recognizing behaviors:

- ❏ By identifying trauma-related behaviors, you can make conscious decisions about your responses in relationships.

Creating triggers and coping strategies list:

- ❏ Example: If you feel anxious when plans change suddenly, practice calming strategies such as:
  - Taking walks
  - Talking to a trusted friend

Aim for Personal Growth:

- ❏ Actionable steps lead to healthier navigation of relationships.

Actionable Steps

_____

_____

_____

_____

Communication With Loved Ones

Expressing feelings:

- ❏ Share feelings and concerns with partners or friends to strengthen relationships.
- ❏ Explain how past experiences might lead to insecurity.

Inviting understanding:

- ❑ Opening up helps invite understanding and support, making it easier for others to be patient and compassionate.
- ❑ Enhances trust, which is essential for healing.

Actionable Steps

_____

_____

_____

Acknowledging Progress

Recognize That Progress Takes Time

- ❑ Expect setbacks; this is completely normal.

Practice Self-Gentleness

- ❑ Celebrate small victories, such as:
    - Handling triggers with healthy responses.
    - Enjoying quiet time alone without fear.

Honor Your Journey

- ❑ Each step toward understanding contributes to healthier emotional patterns.

Actionable Steps

_____

_____

_____

Building a Supportive Community

Surround yourself with support:

- ❑ Find friends or groups who understand trauma for a sense of belonging.

Mutual understanding and healing:

- ❏ Engage in support groups, either in-person or online, to share feelings and strategies.
- ❏ Remind yourself that you are not alone on your journey and that healing is possible.

Actionable Steps

_____

_____

_____

Leading to Substantial Changes

Insight into behavioral symptoms:

- ❏ Recognizing and understanding trauma-related behaviors leads to meaningful life changes.

Path to Healing:

- ❏ Acknowledge avoidance, clinginess, distrust, and emotional sensitivity.
- ❏ Follow awareness with exploration of root causes and therapeutic support.

Empower Through Community:

- ❏ Utilize communication and community support as strengths in your progress.
- ❏ Each small action contributes to healthier relationships and emotional well-being.

Actionable Steps

_____

_____

_____

More Practical Exercises

Explore a variety of engaging exercises designed to reconnect with and nurture your inner child. If you have previously completed any of these exercises, you are welcome to do them again, as our relationships and dynamics change frequently. You may not be at the same stage of your journey as you were when you completed the previous workbooks.

Relationship Pattern Analysis

Objective

To identify and analyze your relationship patterns based on early experiences and attachment styles.

Instructions

Reflect on your past and current relationships. Use the questions below to guide your analysis.

- ❏ Identify relationships in your life (family, friends, romantic). For each relationship, answer the following:
    - What attachment style do you believe you exhibit (secure, anxious, avoidant)?
    - How do you usually react during conflicts in these relationships?
    - Are there recurring themes or behaviors that surface in multiple relationships (e.g., fear of abandonment, withdrawal, or need for reassurance)?
    - What emotions do you feel during conflicts or when you are vulnerable?

_____

_____

_____

After reflecting on these questions, summarize your findings in a table format, outlining the relationship, your attachment style, behaviors, and recurring emotions. This exercise can help you recognize patterns that may have emerged from your childhood experiences.

Guided Journaling

Objective

To enhance self-awareness by identifying triggers related to past trauma that affect your current relationships.

Instructions

Set aside time in a quiet space with your journal. Consider the following prompts and write your thoughts freely.

- ❑ Reflect on a recent situation where you felt overwhelmingly triggered in a relationship. What happened?

- ❑ What specific words, actions, or situations caused this reaction? Were there parallels to past experiences?

- ❑ How did your body react to this trigger? (e.g., tension, avoidance, clammy hands)

- ❑ What thoughts raced through your mind during this reaction?

- ❑ Looking back, how could you have responded differently to this trigger?

Set a timer for 15–20 minutes, and write as much as you can. Afterward, read through your entries to identify any patterns in your triggers and reactions.

_____

_____

_____

Role-Playing Exercises

Objective

To practice assertive communication and boundary-setting in relationships.

Instructions

Pair up with a trusted friend or family member. Take turns playing different roles in the following scenarios.

- ❏ Scenario 1: A friend repeatedly interrupts you during conversations.

    - Role A: The friend who interrupts.

    - Role B: You, expressing your feelings about the interruption and setting boundaries around conversation time.

    - Practice stating your needs assertively, using "I" statements (e.g., "I feel unheard when I am interrupted. I would appreciate it if we could take turns speaking").

- ❏ Scenario 2: A romantic partner expresses dissatisfaction without giving specific feedback.

    - Role A: The partner shares frustrations in a vague manner.

    - Role B: You, practicing clarifying questions and encouraging open dialogue (e.g., "Can you help me understand what specifically is bothering you? I want to address your concerns.").

- ❏ Scenario 3: A family member comments about your relationship choices that make you feel defensive

    - Role A: The family member making the comments.

    - Role B: You, practicing boundary-setting (e.g., "I appreciate your concern, but I need to make my own choices without feeling judged.").

After each role-play, discuss what felt comfortable or challenging. Provide feedback to the other person. Use this space to make notes:

_____

_____

_____

Looking Ahead

As you work through these exercises, notice how your understanding of relationship patterns evolves. In the next chapter, we'll examine recognizing and breaking free from toxic dynamics.

Final Reflection

What's your key takeaway from this chapter?

_____

_____

What practice will you start with tomorrow?

_____

_____

Your Personal Notes

Use this space for additional thoughts and insights:

_____

_____

_____

_____

_____

_____

_____

CHAPTER 2:

Recognizing and Breaking Free from Toxic Dynamics

Recognizing and breaking free from toxic dynamics involves exploring the patterns and behaviors you unconsciously carry from your childhood. Your early experiences shape how you perceive and engage in adult relationships, influencing your boundaries, communication, and emotional responses.

In this chapter, we'll examine various toxic relationship dynamics and their roots in past experiences.

Quick Check-In Exercise

Before we explore toxic relationship dynamics, take a moment to check in with yourself:

Rate your current level (1–10):

❏ Awareness of toxic patterns: _____

❏ Ability to set boundaries: _____

❏ Self-trust in relationships: _____

What relationship dynamics feel most challenging?

_____

What support do you need when addressing difficult patterns?

_____

_____

How do you feel in your body when boundaries are crossed?

___

Exercise: Identifying Red Flags in Toxic Relationships

This exercise will help you identify red flags in your relationships and patterns arising from childhood experiences.

List Red Flags

Write down three red flags you have ignored in your current or past relationships. Examples include:

- ❏ manipulation
- ❏ constant criticism
- ❏ fear of abandonment

___

Reflect on Childhood Experiences

Consider how these red flags may connect to experiences from your childhood. What behaviors did you observe in your family dynamics that resemble these patterns?

___

Evaluating Relationship Impact

Reflect on how these red flags have influenced your ability to establish healthy boundaries. What emotions do you feel when these patterns emerge?

___

Signs of Toxic Relationships

In walking the path to healthier relationships, recognizing red flags is your first step. Toxicity in relationships often manifests through subtle yet pervasive behaviors.

- ❑ Examples include:
    - Manipulation: One partner seeks to control or dominate the other.
    - Constant criticism: Chipping away at your self-worth.

Understanding these patterns allows you to reflect on how such behaviors mirror unresolved dynamics from your formative years.

Paying Attention to Related Triggers

By now you already know that emotional triggers are intense reactions that can derail your communication and relationship harmony. Acknowledging them involves understanding your emotional responses in certain situations. For example, if you were frequently invalidated as a child, you may fear sharing emotions as an adult. Identifying what amplifies these triggers will help you manage your reactions better.

Identifying Codependency to Break Free

Recognize patterns of codependency to break free from toxic dynamics. In codependent relationships, you might excessively rely on your partner for validation. This behavior often stems from childhood environments where self-worth was closely linked to caretaking or seeking approval. Acknowledging these patterns helps you distinguish between healthy support and unhealthy reliance.

Knowing Your Communication Style

Your communication style influences toxic dynamics. Destructive patterns, like passive-aggressiveness or stonewalling, often stem from childhood. Evaluating your communication under stress is vital for learning how to express needs constructively.

Following Practical Guidelines

To effectively address these issues, practical guidelines can offer you direction.

❑ **Reflective journaling:** When considering red flags, keeping a reflective journal helps you track recurring patterns, including feelings that arise during interactions. This practice allows you to spot manipulation or controlling behaviors early. In acknowledging your emotional triggers, mindfulness exercises can assist you in becoming more present and attentive to your emotions as they surface, reducing impulsive reactions.

❑ **Mindfulness techniques:** If you are grappling with codependency, setting small, achievable personal goals outside relational confines can foster your independence. This might include pursuing hobbies or activities alone, which reinforces your self-worth detached from external validation. Addressing your communication styles can benefit greatly from adopting active listening techniques, focusing on understanding before responding. Engaging in open-ended questions encourages dialogue rather than defensive exchanges, promoting healthier discourse.

❑ **Setting goals:** Breaking away from toxic dynamics involves understanding the broader effects these behaviors have on your mental and physical health. Chronic exposure to toxic interactions can lead to stress-related ailments, highlighting the necessity of addressing these issues promptly. Prioritizing your emotional well-being is essential by creating environments that foster open conversation and mutual respect.

❑ **Self-assessment practices:** Introducing regular self-assessment practices aids in maintaining awareness of both your personal growth and relational health. Scheduling time for self-reflection, perhaps weekly, provides you with an opportunity to evaluate your progress and adjust strategies as needed. It is essential to remain patient and compassionate with yourself, as change is gradual and requires consistent effort.

Interactive Exercise: Toxicity-to-Freedom

Take a moment to map your journey from toxic patterns to freedom:

Pattern Recognition

❑ Recurring toxic dynamics: _____
❑ How they show up in my life: _____
❑ What they remind me of from childhood: _____
❑ How I typically respond: _____

Physical and Emotional Signals

- ❑ Body sensations when boundaries are crossed: _____
- ❑ Emotions that arise: _____
- ❑ Thoughts that surface: _____
- ❑ How I typically cope: _____

Freedom Steps

- ❑ Boundaries I need to establish: _____
- ❑ How I'll communicate them: _____
- ❑ Support I need: _____
- ❑ Self-care during this process: _____

Empowerment Plan

- ❑ What freedom from this pattern looks like: _____
- ❑ Small steps I can take today: _____
- ❑ Resources I can access: _____
- ❑ How I'll celebrate progress: _____

Strategies to Confront and Change Negative Cycles

- ❑ Establish boundaries: Clearly define your emotional and physical limits in relationships to safeguard your well-being.
- ❑ Communicate needs: Use "I" statements to express feelings and encourage open discussions.
- ❑ Engage in active listening: Practice understanding your partner's perspective to build empathy and connection.
- ❑ Reflect for awareness: Regularly assess your relationship patterns, using journals to identify triggers and responses.

❑ Patience and persistence: Stay committed to your growth, celebrating progress in breaking negative cycles.

Actionable Steps

_____

_____

_____

Breaking free from these cycles demands courage and commitment. It's about choosing authenticity over comfort, daring to voice needs instead of conforming to past roles, and valuing oneself enough to reject unhealthy patterns. As these skills develop, individuals pave the way for healthier, more fulfilling relationships—not just with others, but also with themselves.

More Interactive Exercises

Explore a variety of engaging exercises designed to reconnect with and nurture your inner child throughout this workbook.

Relationship Pattern Analysis

Objective

To help readers identify and reflect on their relationship patterns stemming from childhood experiences.

Instructions

❑ Take a moment to reflect on your previous relationships. Create two columns: one for positive traits and one for negative traits that you've experienced in those relationships.

❑ Reflect on your childhood and identify any patterns you may have observed in your family dynamics. Write down how these patterns may have influenced your adult relationships.

❑ Answer the following questions in your journal:

- What childhood experiences do you think significantly impacted your adult relationship behaviors?

- Are there specific red flags you recognize in your past relationships that align with those childhood experiences?

- How have these patterns affected your ability to establish boundaries?

___

___

___

___

Guided Journaling

Objective

To facilitate self-reflection and self-awareness regarding emotional triggers and communication styles.

Instructions

- ❏ Dedicate 10–15 minutes daily to journaling this week. Focus on your emotions, interactions, and reactions throughout the day.

- ❏ Use the prompts below to guide your journaling:

    - Describe a situation recently where you felt an intense emotional reaction. What triggered this reaction, and how did you respond?

    - Reflect on your communication style when resolving conflicts. Do you tend to withdraw, become aggressive, or use passive-aggressive methods?

    - Write about a time when you successfully set a boundary. How did it feel, and what was the outcome?

- ❏ At the end of the week, review your journal entries and identify any recurring themes or patterns.

___

___

___

Role-Playing Exercises

Objective

To practice assertive communication and boundary-setting in a safe and constructive environment.

Instructions

- ❑ Pair up with a trusted friend or family member. Take turns playing different roles in the following scenarios:

    - **Scenario 1:** You need to express that a friend frequently cancels plans last minute, affecting your emotional well-being. Practice using "I" statements to express your feelings.

    - **Scenario 2:** You feel overwhelmed with household responsibilities but have trouble asking your partner for help. Role-play how you can assertively communicate your needs.

    - **Scenario 3:** A family member consistently critiques your choices. Role-play how you would set a boundary around these interactions without escalating conflict.

After each role-play, discuss with your partner what felt comfortable and what aspects may require further practice or adjustment.

_____

_____

Looking Ahead

As you work through these exercises, notice how your awareness of toxic dynamics evolves. In the next chapter, we'll explore trusting and communicating effectively to facilitate inner child restoration.

Final Reflection

What's your key takeaway from this chapter?

_____

What practice will you start with tomorrow?

___

___

Your Personal Notes

Use this space for additional thoughts and insights:

___

___

___

___

___

___

___

___

CHAPTER 3:

Trusting and Communicating Effectively

Trust and effective communication are vital in personal relationships. Building lasting connections relies on trusting others and openly expressing thoughts and feelings. Trust acts as a foundation, promoting vulnerability and openness.

Transparent interactions create deeper understanding and empathy, making each person feel heard and respected. Encouraging honesty, partners can tackle challenges more resiliently, leading to stronger bonds. This chapter explores effective communication as a vital tool for emotional clarity, deeper understanding, and empathy, making each person feel heard and respected.

Quick Check-In Exercise

Before we explore trust and communication, take a moment to check in with yourself:

Rate your current level (1–10):

- ❏ Trust in relationships: _____
- ❏ Communication comfort: _____
- ❏ Ability to express needs: _____

What makes communication feel safe?
_____

What barriers do you face when trying to be open?
_____

What would help you communicate more effectively?

_____

_____

Building Trust Through Transparency

Transparency in relationships is essential for building trust through open sharing of thoughts and feelings, creating a secure bond.

- ❑ **Open communication:** Sharing feelings about work stress allows your partner to understand your emotional state, fostering empathy and support. This insight can prevent misunderstandings, leading to solutions that strengthen your bond.
- ❑ **Regular dialogue:** Engaging in ongoing conversations about expectations reinforces trust. Regular check-ins reaffirm commitment and enhance reliability, making both partners aware of evolving needs.
- ❑ **Weekly discussions:** Setting aside time each week for discussions about challenges—whether family, financial, or personal—aligns your goals and helps avoid conflicts. This communication rhythm fosters stability and predictability.
- ❑ **The role of honesty:** Honesty is the foundation of genuine connections. Being truthful reinforces credibility and respect, allowing open dialogues where both partners feel safe to express themselves without judgment.
- ❑ **Embracing mistakes:** Admitting mistakes can change your relationship's trajectory. While it may introduce discomfort, it leads to growth and understanding, replacing tension with mutual respect.
- ❑ **Navigating vulnerability:** Sharing personal experiences promotes emotional intimacy and understanding triggers. Discussing past traumas helps partners provide individualized support without exacerbating emotional wounds, creating a more empathetic connection.

Openness promotes mutual understanding and a strengthened connection, ensuring both partners feel seen and heard.

Exercise: Building Trust Through Transparency

Objective

To enhance trust within your relationships by practicing transparency.

Instructions

Identify Trust Levels

❑ Reflect on your current relationships. Write down:

- A partner or friend you trust deeply.
- Someone you find it difficult to trust.

_____

_____

Assess Trust Factors

❑ For the trusted individual:

- What specific actions or qualities contribute to your trust in them?

❑ For the individual you find difficult to trust:

- What behaviors make you hesitant?

_____

_____

Enhance Openness

❑ Consider areas where you might improve transparency with the trusted individual. Write down three specific ways to foster openness:

_____

_____

Communicate Your Thoughts

❑ Plan to discuss these thoughts with the trusted individual. Prepare what you'd like to say to encourage dialogue:

_____

_____

Effective Communication Techniques for Emotional Clarity

Effective communication is a cornerstone of healthy relationships, enabling you to connect on a deeper level.

- ❏ Active listening involves fully engaging and understanding emotions.
- ❏ Feeling heard strengthens trust and validates experiences.
- ❏ Show true interest by resisting interruptions and acknowledging feelings.
- ❏ Use "I" statements to express personal feelings and reduce defensiveness.
- ❏ Clarifying intentions eliminates confusion by outlining discussion goals.
- ❏ Practicing empathy connects with the emotions behind words and fosters understanding.
- ❏ Empathetic communication creates a supportive environment for honest expression.

Actionable Steps

_____

_____

_____

Interactive Exercise: Communication Style Assessment

Take a moment to map your communication patterns:

Communication Strengths

- ❏ When I communicate best: _____
- ❏ Topics I discuss easily: _____
- ❏ My positive communication traits: _____
- ❏ How others respond when I'm at my best: _____

Communication Challenges

- ❑ Topics I avoid: _____
- ❑ When I tend to shut down: _____
- ❑ Communication patterns I learned as a child: _____
- ❑ What triggers defensiveness: _____

Listening Assessment

- ❑ How I show I'm listening: _____
- ❑ Distractions I notice: _____
- ❑ My understanding patterns: _____
- ❑ How I can improve: _____

Trust Building Plan

- ❑ How I want to be more transparent: _____
- ❑ Relationships I want to strengthen: _____
- ❑ Small steps I can take: _____
- ❑ How I'll track progress: _____

More Practical Exercises

Explore a variety of engaging exercises designed to reconnect with and nurture your inner child throughout this workbook.

Trust-Building Reflection

Objective

To help you assess your trust levels in relationships and identify ways to enhance trust through transparency.

Instructions

- ❑ Reflect on your current relationships. Write down a partner or friend you trust deeply and one you find it difficult to trust.

- ❏ For each individual, answer the following questions in your journal:
    - What specific actions or behaviors contribute to your trust in them?
    - Conversely, what makes you hesitant to trust the other person?
- ❏ Consider the importance of transparency and write down three areas where you could improve openness with your trusted individual. How can you communicate these thoughts?

_____

_____

_____

_____

Active Listening Practice

Objective

To develop active listening skills in everyday conversations.

Instructions

- ❏ Pair up with a friend or family member. Each person should take turns sharing a story or experience for five minutes without interruption.
- ❏ The listener should practice active listening, using the following techniques:
    - Maintain eye contact and nod to show engagement.
    - After the speaker finishes, paraphrase what they shared to confirm understanding. For example, "So what I'm hearing is..."
- ❏ Discuss how it felt to be either the speaker or the listener. Reflect on how this practice impacted the emotional depth of the conversation.

_____

_____

_____

_____

"I" Statement Exercise

Objective

To practice using "I" statements to foster effective communication.

Instructions

- ❏ Write down three common situations where you experience frustration or conflict in your relationships.

- ❏ For each situation, rephrase your feelings using "I" statements instead of accusatory language. For example:

    - Instead of "You never listen to me," write, "I feel unheard when my thoughts aren't acknowledged."

- ❏ Role-play these scenarios with a partner, practicing your "I" statements. Afterward, ask for feedback on how the communication felt compared to past experiences without using "I" statements.

_____

_____

_____

Intentional Conversations Checklist

Objective

To prepare for meaningful discussions that clarify intentions and goals.

Instructions

- ❏ Identify a topic you want to discuss with a partner (e.g., future plans, emotional needs, or any concerns).

- ❏ Create a checklist to guide your conversation preparation:

    - What is the main goal of this conversation?
    - How can I frame my thoughts clearly?
    - What potential misunderstandings should I address upfront?
    - How can I demonstrate empathy during the conversation?

❑ After having the conversation, reflect on its outcomes. Did setting intentions improve the clarity and understanding between you and your partner?

_____
_____
_____

Looking Ahead

As you work through these exercises, notice how your trust and communication abilities evolve. In the next chapter, we'll discuss how to foster emotional vulnerability and authentic connections.

Final Reflection

What's your key takeaway from this chapter?

_____
_____

What practice will you start with tomorrow?

_____
_____

Your Personal Notes

Use this space for additional thoughts and insights:

_____
_____
_____
_____
_____

CHAPTER 4:

Encouraging Emotional Vulnerability and Authentic Connections

Emotional vulnerability is the foundation for authentic connections in any relationship. It allows us to reveal our true selves to others, fostering trust and intimacy.

The chapter explores various elements that contribute to nurturing emotional openness and authenticity in relationships.

Quick Check-In Exercise

Before we explore emotional vulnerability, take a moment to check in with yourself:

Rate your current level (1–10):

- ❏ Comfort with vulnerability: _____
- ❏ Authenticity in relationships: _____
- ❏ Ability to express emotions: _____

What emotions are most difficult to express?

_____

_____

What helps you feel safe being vulnerable?

_____

_____

What benefits have you experienced from sharing authentically?

_____

_____

Encouraging Emotional Vulnerability

Emotional vulnerability is often misunderstood as a weakness when, in reality, it serves as the foundation for authentic connections. To truly connect with another person, you must allow yourself to be seen as you are—unshielded and genuine. This openness invites deeper engagement and strengthens relational bonds, creating an atmosphere where authenticity thrives.

Positive Affirmation

"I am brave enough to show my true self and trust in the connections I create."

Action Step

Identify one small thing you can share with someone today that feels vulnerable. It could be a fear, an insecurity, or even a desire.

_____

_____

_____

Establishing a Safe Space

Creating a safe space is crucial for fostering trust and openness with others. A safe space is characterized by an environment where you feel secure in expressing your emotions without fear of criticism or judgment. Here, you can share your innermost thoughts and feelings confidently, knowing that your vulnerabilities will be met with understanding and acceptance.

Positive Affirmation

"I deserve to feel safe and supported when I share my feelings."

Action Step

Communicate your need for a safe space with someone you trust. Outline what makes you feel secure during conversations and invite them to share their needs as well.

_____

_____

_____

Balancing Openness and Boundaries

Boundaries play an essential role in nurturing an environment for vulnerability. While emotional vulnerability requires openness, it also benefits from the structure that boundaries provide. Establishing clear boundaries ensures that your emotional landscape is respected, allowing both parties to express their needs and desires safely.

Positive Affirmation

"I set healthy boundaries that honor my needs and promote mutual respect."

Action Step

Reflect on one boundary you can establish in your relationships. Write it down and practice how you will communicate this boundary to others.

_____

_____

_____

The Importance of Intentional Check-ins

Intentional check-ins are vital tools for maintaining the strength of emotional connections. These moments allow you to discuss feelings and address any concerns that may arise. Regular check-ins create opportunities for ongoing communication and prevent issues from festering unchecked.

Positive Affirmation

"I value open communication, and I am committed to nurturing my relationships."

Action Step

Schedule a specific time with a loved one for a check-in conversation this week. Prepare topics you want to discuss, focusing on emotions and experiences.

___

___

___

Guidelines for Effective Check-ins

Effective check-ins involve ensuring both parties are prepared to listen and share openly. This practice keeps communication pathways clear, allowing emotions to flow freely and deepening the bond.

Positive Affirmation

"I approach conversations with openness and a willingness to listen."

Action Step

Create a short checklist of questions to guide your check-in conversation, such as:

- ❑ How have you been feeling lately?
- ❑ Is there anything on your mind that you'd like to share?

___

___

___

Celebrating Vulnerability

Celebrating vulnerability acknowledges its value and fosters closeness between you and others. Recognizing the bravery it takes to share deeply personal experiences reinforces trust and encourages openness.

Positive Affirmation

"I honor vulnerability as a strength that strengthens my connections."

Action Step

After someone shares something vulnerable with you, make a point to acknowledge their openness with gratitude. A simple "Thank you for trusting me with that" can strengthen your bond.

___

___

___

The Power of Authenticity

Feeling celebrated for your authenticity encourages continued openness, leading to meaningful interactions. Acknowledging vulnerability can pave the way for deeper understanding and empathy.

Positive Affirmation

"I embrace my authentic self, and I recognize the beauty in my vulnerabilities."

Action Step

Reflect on a recent instance where you felt authentic in sharing your feelings. Journal about how that moment felt and how it affected your relationship with the other person.

___

___

___

Developing emotional vulnerability is about creating an environment where openness is met with respect, compassion, and care. As you nurture this practice, remember that it transforms relationships from surface-level interactions into profound connections where both individuals can grow and thrive together.

Interactive Exercise: Vulnerability Building Blocks

Take a moment to map your journey toward greater vulnerability:

Vulnerability Inventory

- ❏ Areas where I'm already vulnerable: _____
- ❏ Emotions I express easily: _____
- ❏ Topics I find difficult to discuss: _____
- ❏ People I feel safest with: _____

Safety Assessment

- ❏ What helps me feel emotionally safe: _____
- ❏ What makes me shut down: _____
- ❏ Physical signs I'm closing off: _____
- ❏ How I can signal my needs: _____

Expression Practice

- ❏ Low-risk share to practice: _____
- ❏ Medium-risk share to try: _____
- ❏ How I'll prepare myself: _____
- ❏ Support I need afterward: _____

Connection Blueprint

- ❏ Relationships I want to deepen: _____
- ❏ First small step with each person : _____
- ❏ How I'll invite vulnerability: _____
- ❏ How I'll respond to others' openness: _____

Practicing Emotional Vulnerability in Intimate Relationships

While vulnerability can feel uncomfortable, developing this skill is essential for deeper and more meaningful relationships. Here are six practical ways to practice emotional vulnerability, along with activities to enhance your experience.

Connect With Your Partner Regularly

Emotional check-ins shouldn't wait for a crisis. Make it a habit to ask your partner about their feelings, thoughts, and experiences in everyday life. This proactive approach shows you genuinely care and creates a safe space for vulnerability.

Activity: Daily Connection Ritual

Set aside 10–15 minutes each day for a "connection chat" with your partner. Choose a comfortable environment, like sitting together on the couch or during a walk.

During this time, each share:

- ❑ One thing that made you happy today.
- ❑ One concern or thought that's been on your mind.

This practice will help build emotional intimacy and strengthen your bond.

_____

_____

_____

Learn From Vulnerable Role Models

Look around and identify people in your life who are comfortable expressing their emotions. Notice how they do it—what words they use, their tone, and how others respond to them.

Activity: Role Model Reflection

- ❑ Write down the names of two or three vulnerable role models in your life.
- ❑ Reflect on a time when you admired their openness. What specifically did they do that inspired you?
- ❑ Consider how you can incorporate similar behaviors into your own life

_____

_____

_____

Go Slow and Take Your Time

Vulnerability can feel intimidating, especially if you've guarded yourself for a long time. It's essential to take gradual steps toward opening up.

Activity: Vulnerability Ladder

- ❑ Create a "vulnerability ladder" where you list small, medium, and large disclosures you'd feel comfortable sharing with your partner.
- ❑ Start with simple fears or concerns in the small section.
    - Progress to more personal stories or insecurities in the medium section.
    - Aim for significant experiences or feelings in the large section.
- ❑ Each week, choose one item from the next level to share, respecting your pace.

_____

_____

_____

Acknowledge Your Feelings

Recognizing your emotions is the first step in practicing vulnerability. When you feel intense emotions arising, take a moment to identify what you're feeling instead of shutting down or jumping into problem-solving mode.

Activity: Feelings Check-In

- ❑ Keep a feelings journal for a week. Each time you notice strong emotions, pause and jot down:
    - what you're feeling (e.g., angry, scared, excited).
    - what triggered this emotion.
    - how you responded to it (e.g., avoidance, opening up).

Reflect at the end of the week on any patterns you observe in your feelings and responses.

_____

_____

_____

Share Personal Stories

Sharing meaningful experiences from your past can deepen your emotional connections. Discuss moments from childhood, challenges you've faced, and your hopes for the future. Being open about your fears and insecurities paves the way for mutual understanding.

Activity: Storytelling Sessions

- ❑ Plan a dedicated time for sharing stories with your partner. Each person can take turns sharing a significant memory or experience.

- ❑ As you share, focus on your emotions during the event; it's not just about the story, but how it shaped you.

- ❑ After each story, discuss what resonated most with you and how it strengthens your understanding of one another.

_____

_____

_____

Practice Empathy

Being open to your partner's vulnerabilities is vital for emotional intimacy. When they share, listen attentively without judgment. Acknowledge their feelings, even if you don't fully agree with their perspective.

Activity: Empathy Exercise

- ❑ During your next conversation about feelings, practice reflecting back what your partner shares. For example, say, "It sounds like you're feeling overwhelmed because of work. Can you tell me more?"

- ❑ After the conversation, jot down your thoughts on how this practice felt and what impact it had on your connection.

_____

_____

_____

Practicing Empathy and Authentic Interactions

Empathy is a cornerstone of meaningful relationships, enabling deeper emotional connections. It involves awareness and acknowledgment of another person's feelings and perspectives, fostering mutual understanding and respect. Empathetic interactions create genuine and resilient bonds, allowing each person to feel seen and valued for who they truly are.

Positive Affirmation

"I am capable of understanding others' emotions and creating meaningful connections."

Action Step

Take a moment today to check in with someone in your life—ask them how they are feeling and practice active listening during the conversation.

_____

_____

_____

The Power of Empathy in Communication

When empathy is present, it enhances communication and understanding. You can share your inner experiences without fear of being misunderstood or judged. This shared understanding creates a fertile ground for authentic connections, encouraging full self-expression and leading to enriching and enduring relationships.

Positive Affirmation

"My emotions are valid, and I can express them openly with those I trust."

Action Step

Identify one person you feel safe with and share a personal experience or feeling you've been holding onto. Allow yourself to be vulnerable in this interaction.

_____

_____

_____

The Importance of Active Listening

Active listening is a vital technique for cultivating an empathetic environment. It goes beyond simply hearing words; it requires full attentiveness and engagement in the conversation. When you practice active listening, you show your partner that their thoughts and feelings are valued.

Positive Affirmation

"I listen with intention, understanding that my presence matters."

Action Step

During your next conversation, focus on being fully present—put away distractions, maintain eye contact, and respond with nods. After they finish speaking, summarize what they said to show you were actively listening.

_____

_____

Guidelines for Effective Listening

Implementing effective listening strategies can significantly boost relationship dynamics.

- ❑ **Eliminate Distractions:** Focus your attention solely on the speaker.
- ❑ **Practice Reflective Listening:** Paraphrase what the speaker has said to confirm your understanding.
- ❑ **Ask Open-Ended Questions:** Encourage deeper sharing and emotional exploration.

Positive Affirmation

"I create a safe space for others to express their thoughts and feelings."

Action Step

Choose a conversation where you can ask open-ended questions. Prepare a few questions ahead of time to facilitate deeper discussion.

_____

_____

The Role of Authenticity in Emotional Connections

Authenticity is vital for fostering emotional connections through transparent communication. When you share your personal thoughts and feelings, you lay the groundwork for trust, revealing your true self to others.

Positive Affirmation

"I embrace my authentic self and communicate openly with those I care about."

Action Step

Identify one area where you can be more authentic in your conversations. It could be discussing your true feelings about a project or sharing a personal goal with a friend.

_____

_____

The Benefits of Vulnerability

To communicate authentically, you must be willing to be vulnerable and take risks in disclosing your thoughts and emotions. This openness often leads to stronger ties and deeper companionship.

Positive Affirmation

"Being vulnerable is a strength that fosters deeper relationships."

Action Step

Reflect on a vulnerable feeling you have been avoiding. Share it with a trusted friend or partner, and explore how they respond.

_____

_____

Responding with Compassion

Compassionate responses serve as affirmations of understanding, encouraging vulnerability. When you acknowledge someone's feelings without judgment, you create a safe space for emotional expression.

Positive Affirmation

"I respond compassionately to both myself and others."

Action Step

The next time someone shares a difficult feeling, take a moment to validate their experience. Respond with phrases like, "That sounds really tough" or "I understand how you feel."

_____

_____

The Power of Compassionate Engagement

Engaging compassionately changes relationships into sanctuaries for emotional growth. These interactions allow you to confront and process complex emotions together, fostering healing and resilience.

Positive Affirmation

"Compassion strengthens my relationships and encourages open communication."

Action Step

Plan a dedicated time this week to have a heartfelt conversation with a loved one about feelings and vulnerabilities. Use this time to express support for each other.

_____

_____

Incorporating empathy, active listening, authenticity, and compassion into our interactions encourages deeper and more meaningful relationships

More Practical Exercises

Explore a variety of engaging exercises designed to reconnect with and nurture your inner child throughout this workbook.

Building Authentic Connection Activities

Creating Safe Spaces

Objective

To help readers identify and establish safe environments for emotional expression in their relationships.

Instructions

- ❑ Reflect on your current relationships and identify one person with whom you would like to enhance emotional openness.

- ❑ Write a list of characteristics that would make you feel safe sharing your vulnerabilities with them. For example, consider traits like non-judgmental attitude, supportive responses, and consistency.

- ❑ Discuss with this person how you can create a safe space together. Propose specific practices, such as setting aside time for open conversations or agreeing to support each other's emotional needs without interruption.

_____

_____

_____

Intentional Check-ins

Objective

To implement regular check-ins with partners or close friends to maintain emotional connection.

Instructions

- ❑ Schedule a weekly or biweekly check-in with someone you value.
- ❑ Prepare a simple structure for these conversations by writing down key questions you want to address, such as:
    - How are you feeling about our relationship lately?
    - Are there any concerns you'd like to discuss?
    - What can I do to support you better?

❑ After the first check-in, reflect on the experience in your journal. Consider what went well and what could be improved for future discussions.

Practicing Active Listening

Objective

To develop active listening skills that deepen connections.

Instructions

❑ Pair up with a friend or family member. Designate one person as the speaker and the other as the listener for five-minute intervals.

❑ The listener should focus on practicing active listening techniques: maintain eye contact, avoid distractions, and respond with nods and affirmations.

❑ After the speaker finishes, the listener should summarize what they heard and share their reflections on the emotions conveyed.

❑ Switch roles and repeat the exercise. Conclude by discussing how active listening affected the quality of the conversation and your feelings of connection.

Celebrating Vulnerability

Objective

To acknowledge and celebrate the vulnerability shared in relationships.

Instructions

❑ Reflect on a time when someone shared something vulnerable with you. Write down what you appreciated about their openness.

❏ Create a simple plan to celebrate vulnerability in your interactions. For example, actively thank your partner or friend after they share something personal, and express how their trust impacts your relationship positively.

❏ Try to implement this celebration of vulnerability at least once in the coming week. Journal about the experience and how it affected your connection.

___

Looking Ahead

As you work through these exercises, notice how your capacity for vulnerability and authentic connection evolves. In the next chapter, we'll explore building strong and healthy relationships.

Final Reflection

What's your key takeaway from this chapter?

___

What practice will you start with tomorrow?

___

Your Personal Notes

Use this space for additional thoughts and insights:

___

CHAPTER 5:

Building Strong, Healthy Relationships

Building strong, healthy relationships is a multifaceted endeavor centered on mutual respect and understanding. Relationships serve as the cornerstone of our interpersonal experience, shaping much of how we navigate the world around us.

This chapter explores the essentials that form the backbone of thriving connections, aiming to help you develop relationships that are lasting and truly fulfilling. Particularly for those who have grappled with childhood wounds, understanding these dynamics can offer a path to healing and transformation. As you explore your relational patterns, the insights provided here pave the way toward building a foundation of trust and appreciation, cornerstones of any meaningful bond.

Quick Check-In Exercise

Before we explore building healthy relationships, take a moment to check in with yourself:

Rate your current level (1–10):

- ❏ Satisfaction with relationships: _____
- ❏ Ability to set boundaries: _____
- ❏ Communication effectiveness: _____

What qualities do you value most in relationships?

_____

_____

What relationship patterns would you like to change?

_____

_____

_____

What makes you feel most appreciated in relationships?

_____

_____

_____

Foundations of a Healthy Relationship

Developing strong, healthy relationships involves understanding and integrating several foundational elements. At the heart of these components are mutual respect and understanding—essential ingredients that enable partners to connect on a deeper level, fostering lasting bonds.

Trust: The Cornerstone of Your Relationship

Trust isn't merely a passive element but an active process requiring continuous nurturing. Prioritizing transparency and honesty, you lay a firm groundwork for open communication, which is vital for meaningful connections. Trust allows you to share vulnerabilities without fear of judgment or ridicule, fostering an environment where you can truly be yourself.

For example, when you feel comfortable expressing doubts or desires, it opens the door to discussions that deepen mutual understanding and strengthen the bond. Encouraging small acts of dependability, like keeping promises or being there during challenging times, builds a track record of reliability that cements trust further. As such, one guideline for establishing trust is to ensure consistency in your actions and words, demonstrating that both you and your partner are committed to maintaining openness and truthfulness in every interaction.

Positive Affirmation

"I trust my partner completely, and we continuously nurture our bond."

Action Step

Schedule regular check-ins to discuss any feelings of uncertainty or doubt.

Appreciating Differences

Respecting personal differences is vital for relational growth. Every person brings a unique set of experiences, perspectives, and choices to a relationship. Recognizing these differences does not imply merely tolerating them; instead, it's about valuing the diversity they bring and seeing them as opportunities for enrichment.

When you and your partner celebrate these distinct traits, you foster an atmosphere of acceptance that promotes harmony and reduces conflicts. For instance, engaging in activities that highlight each other's strengths or learning from differing viewpoints can transform potential disagreements into opportunities for growth. In doing so, you create a dynamic where differences are not seen as obstacles but as assets contributing to a more vibrant and adaptable relationship ecosystem.

Positive Affirmation

"I cherish our unique differences, as they enrich our relationship."

Action Step

Set aside time each week to share something new you learned about each other's perspectives.

Providing Emotional Support

Emotional support goes beyond offering comfort during crises—it involves recognizing and validating each other's feelings continually. By acknowledging emotions, you affirm each other's importance and demonstrate empathy, which helps cultivate a sense of safety within the relationship.

For instance, regularly checking in on each other's emotional well-being and offering a listening ear whenever needed reinforces the idea that you and your partner are valued and cared for. Consistent emotional affirmation fosters a safe space where you both feel encouraged to be vulnerable and open, knowing you will be met with compassion and understanding. Another guideline here is to actively practice emotional listening, ensuring that each of you feels heard and understood, thereby enhancing the feeling of belonging.

Positive Affirmation

"I am always here to support my partner emotionally."

Action Step

Initiate a weekly emotional check-in where both partners can share thoughts and feelings freely.

_____

_____

_____

_____

Aligning on Key Values

When you and your partner share fundamental beliefs and priorities, it fosters collaboration toward common goals. This alignment provides a framework for decision-making, minimizing friction and misunderstandings from differing aspirations.

Discussing long-term intentions about career paths, family planning, or lifestyle choices helps identify shared values early, creating a united approach to future challenges. As partners strive for these collective goals, they build a resilient union rooted in shared purpose.

To reinforce shared values, regularly engage in conversations about future visions, adjust plans collaboratively, and celebrate small achievements together.

Positive Affirmation

"We are aligned in our values and work together toward our goals."

Action Step

Schedule monthly discussions to revisit and align on your shared values and goals.

_____

_____

Interactive Exercise: Relationship Blueprint

Take a moment to design your ideal relationship foundations:

Core Values Assessment

- ❏ Values I need in relationships: _____
- ❏ Non-negotiable principles: _____
- ❏ What mutual respect looks like to me: _____
- ❏ How I express my values: _____

Trust-Building Plan

- ❏ How I demonstrate trustworthiness: _____
- ❏ Signs of trust in others: _____
- ❏ Trust barriers I've experienced: _____
- ❏ Steps to rebuild broken trust: _____

Support Exchange

- ❏ How I prefer to receive support: _____
- ❏ How I like to offer support: _____
- ❏ Support I need but rarely ask for: _____
- ❏ Best ways to communicate needs: _____

Relationship Maintenance

- ❏ Regular check-ins I want to establish: _____

❑ Conflict resolution approach: _____

❑ Special rituals to maintain connection: _____

❑ Growth opportunities to pursue together: _____

Nurturing Relationships Through Consistency and Commitment

Consistency and commitment are the cornerstones of any thriving relationship. In the hustle and bustle of modern life, establishing routines can bring about a sense of stability and predictability that is often missing in your daily interactions. When you engage in regular activities together—whether it's a weekly date night, morning coffee rituals, or weekend hikes — these shared experiences create a comforting rhythm. This routine offers reassurance in uncertain times and helps to build trust over time.

Knowing what to expect from another person reduces anxiety and crafts a space for both people to be themselves.

Positive Affirmation

"Our consistent connections strengthen our bond and bring joy to our lives."

Action Step

Schedule at least one regular activity each week to enjoy together.

_____

_____

Commitment to Growth

Beyond the surface level of togetherness, your commitment to personal and relational growth plays a pivotal role in maintaining healthy connections. Relationships thrive when both you and your partner are willing to learn and grow together. This growth mindset can manifest in numerous ways, such as taking a class together, pursuing a mutual hobby, or simply being open to constructive feedback.

Positive Affirmation

"We are always evolving, and our relationship flourishes as we grow together."

Action Step

Choose one new activity or learning opportunity to explore together this month.

_____

_____

Constructive Conflict Resolution

Despite every effort to maintain harmony, conflicts are inevitable. However, addressing disagreements constructively can significantly influence the health of your relationship. Approaching conflicts with empathy means truly listening to understand your partner's perspective, rather than just waiting for your turn to speak. Empathy allows you to connect on an emotional level, transforming potential disputes into opportunities for deeper understanding and cooperation. Constructive conflict resolution avoids escalation by focusing on solutions that honor both of your feelings and needs.

Positive Affirmation

Our differences enhance our connection, and we can resolve conflicts with love and understanding.

Action Step

Practice active listening during your next disagreement and summarize your partner's perspective before responding.

_____

_____

Practical Guidelines

Guidelines can further support these aspects. For establishing routines, consider creating a weekly schedule that includes time for shared activities. Use digital calendars to set reminders, ensuring that these moments are prioritized despite busy schedules. For your commitment to growth, you might choose to regularly assess your relationship goals and discuss areas where you'd like to improve together. This could include setting aside time each month for meaningful conversation or engaging in activities that challenge personal limits and promote learning.

Positive Affirmation

We prioritize our relationship by making intentional choices together.

Action Step

Set up a shared calendar or planner to plan and reflect on your routines and goals.

_____

_____

Milestone Acknowledgment

When celebrating milestones, it's helpful to keep a journal or digital repository of achievements and memories. Photos, notes, or simple entries capturing joyful moments can be revisited to remind you of your shared journey. Acknowledging these milestones doesn't always have to be grand; even a heartfelt message or a small token can convey appreciation and strengthen your bonds.

Positive Affirmation

We cherish our shared memories, which deepen our love and connection.

Action Step

Create a scrapbook or digital album to document and celebrate your relationship milestones.

_____

_____

Conflict Management Strategies

In managing conflicts with care, you may benefit from laying down ground rules before disagreements arise. Agreeing to pause and cool off if tempers flare or committing to expressing grievances without blaming language can prevent misunderstandings. Practice active listening exercises, allowing both of you to voice your thoughts fully before responding. A collaborative approach to resolving conflicts encourages a culture of respect and paves the way for honest and open communication.

Positive Affirmation

Our commitment to respectful conflict management strengthens our partnership.

Action Step

Establish a set of ground rules for discussing conflicts and practice them regularly.

More Practical Exercises

Explore a variety of engaging exercises designed to reconnect with and nurture your inner child throughout this workbook.

Trust Assessment and Development

Objective

To help readers evaluate and enhance the level of trust in their relationships.

Instructions

- ❑ Reflect on your relationships and rate the level of trust you feel in each on a scale from 1 to 10.
- ❑ For relationships rated lower than 7, identify specific actions that betray trust, such as broken promises or lack of transparency. Write these down.
- ❑ Now, create a list of small, consistent actions you can take to build trust in these relationships (e.g., keeping commitments, being honest about feelings). Commit to implementing at least one of these actions in the coming week.

_____

_____

_____

Embracing Individual Differences Exercise

Objective

To appreciate and celebrate the unique traits in your relationships.

Instructions

- ❑ Choose a partner or close friend and write down three qualities you admire in them that are distinct from your own. Reflect on why these differences are valuable.

- ❑ Plan a conversation with this person to celebrate their unique traits. Express what you appreciate about their perspectives and experiences.

- ❑ After the conversation, journal about how recognizing these differences has influenced your relationship and how it can foster a more enriched connection.

Emotional Support Check-in

Objective

To establish a routine of emotional support through intentional check-ins.

Instructions

- ❑ Schedule a weekly emotional check-in with a significant person in your life. Write down three questions you would like to ask them about their emotional well-being.

- ❑ During the check-in, practice active listening: give them your full attention, avoid interruptions, and refrain from judgment while they share their feelings.

- ❑ After the conversation, reflect in your journal about how this check-in impacted your connection and if there are any feelings or issues that require follow-up.

Looking Ahead

As you work through these exercises, notice how your approach to relationships evolves. This concludes our exploration through the Inner Child Relationships workbook. Remember that healing and growth are ongoing journeys, and each step you take builds a stronger foundation for healthy connections.

Final Reflection

What's your key takeaway from this chapter?

_____
_____
_____

What relationship practice will you start with tomorrow?

_____
_____
_____

Your Personal Notes

Use this space for additional thoughts and insights:

_____
_____
_____
_____
_____
_____
_____

CONCLUSION

If this journey into understanding and healing, reflect on how childhood experiences profoundly shape adult relationships. The core of our emotional life stems from these formative years, influencing behaviors and interactions often unconsciously. Recognizing how early wounds affect our present is both challenging and enlightening, marking a significant step toward personal growth and healing.

These experiences can hinder our ability to trust and connect deeply. This acknowledgment isn't about lingering in the past; it's about empowering ourselves to progress more consciously. Understanding childhood trauma's role in our relationships offers insights that promote genuine transformation.

Breaking free from toxic patterns is critical in this process. Many repeat unhealthy dynamics, mirroring unresolved issues from the past. Self-awareness is essential in identifying these patterns, recognizing red flags in interactions.

Awareness leads to action, which drives change. Actively disrupting negative patterns opens avenues to healthier relationships. This involves setting boundaries and sometimes distancing from unhelpful relationships, creating environments where positive connections can thrive.

Effective communication is vital for improving relationships influenced by childhood wounds. Mastering clear, empathetic communication fosters emotional clarity. Using "I" statements enhances understanding and invites collaboration, turning confrontational exchanges into opportunities for connection.

Embracing emotional vulnerability is essential for deeper intimacy and trust. Creating a space for vulnerability involves patience and sensitivity, respecting emotional landscapes, and encouraging openness without judgment. Ultimately, this journey offers actionable steps, prioritizing self-care and self-acceptance while actively working on healthier connections grounded in authenticity, empathy, and love. Healing is about embracing wholeness and navigating life compassionately.

Thank you for allowing this book to be part of your journey toward healing and self-discovery. As you step into the future, join me in our final guide, Authentic Self Workbook: Transform Your Life With Daily Practices to Embrace Confidence, Joy, and Inner Fulfillment.

BOOK 5

Authentic Self Workbook

Transform Your Life with Daily Practices to Embrace Confidence, Joy, and Inner Fulfillment

INTRODUCTION

In our fast-moving world, where self-doubt lurks around every corner, finding a sense of authentic self can feel elusive. Yet, each twist and turn of life's journey holds the potential for transformation and deeper fulfillment. Imagine standing in front of a mirror, preparing for a new chapter—a job, a relationship, or simply a new day. In those moments, you may confront anxiety or uncertainty, questioning your ability to face what lies ahead. Picture taking a deep breath, filled not just with air but with the confidence you've cultivated from uncovering your true self. This scenario can be your reality.

Our journey begins here, with the promise of profound personal growth and a nurturing environment for self-love. This workbook is a gateway to rediscovering who you are and creating a life brimming with purpose. Through thoughtfully curated daily practices, you'll embrace your strengths, acknowledge your vulnerabilities, and step boldly into a life where you flourish as your true self.

Have you wondered how to reconnect with your true self after emotional challenges or pondered what daily practices could nurture self-love and confidence? This book answers these questions, equipping you with practical tools for daily reflection and action. The exercises are designed to enhance your understanding of personal authenticity and empower you to build emotional resilience—an area where many self-help resources fall short.

Imagine feeling confident and joyful as you navigate relationships, knowing you possess the strength to face uncertainties. Engaging with this workbook will shift how you perceive yourself and interact with the world around you. Each day, you'll uncover layers of yourself hidden by years of self-doubt and external expectations.

Now is the moment to take charge of your destiny and transform unfulfillment into growth opportunities. Each day spent disconnected from your authentic self is a day of unrealized potential and joy. Through my struggles, I've experienced the high walls of insecurity and doubt. Refusing to accept these challenges as part of my identity allowed me to discover practices that reshaped my life.

My goal is to offer support and guidance, demonstrating that transformation and healing are within reach. Your struggles do not define your worth or limit your capacity for joy; rather, they serve as stepping stones to a richer life.

The key chapters systematically guide you through the process of embracing your inner self:

1) **Rediscovering Your Authentic Self After Healing**
2) **Cultivating Daily Practices for Self-Love and Confidence**
3) **Embracing Joy and Playfulness in Everyday Life**
4) **Sustaining Inner Peace Through Personal Growth**
5) **The Ongoing Journey to Wholeness**

Each exercise in this workbook is designed to enhance self-awareness and clarify your life's purpose. Engage wholeheartedly with them, seeing them as invitations to embrace who you are and who you aspire to be. Approach these exercises with openness, so you emerge stronger and more aligned with your unique potential.

Your story is important, and as you navigate this journey, remember you are not alone. Many others seek the same peace and authenticity. Together, we create a movement of empowerment, supporting each other's growth.

Investing in yourself now, you're opening up a future filled with possibilities. Understand that transformation is not linear; it ebbs and flows, but every small step forward matters. With compassion and commitment, you will shift not just your perspective but also how you live each moment.

Let's continue on this adventure of self-discovery, illuminating the path toward the life you envision. Welcome to your journey of transformation.

CHAPTER 1:

Rediscovering Your Authentic Self After Healing

Rediscovering your authentic self is a journey of removing the layers formed from past experiences. Your identity can become obscured by the expectations, judgments, and stories imposed by yourself and others over time. These external influences may cause you to adopt false personas that don't reflect your true self, often as a way to protect or adapt to your surroundings. Unraveling these layers requires conscious effort but offers the reward of living more fully and genuinely.

In this chapter, you will explore how past experiences shape your view of authenticity and learn strategies for healing and reconnecting.

Quick Check-In Exercise

Before we explore your authentic self, take a moment to check in with yourself:

Rate your current level (1–10):

- ❏ Connection with your authentic self: _____
- ❏ Freedom from past conditioning: _____
- ❏ Self-expression in daily life: _____

What aspects of yourself feel most authentic?

_____

_____

What masks do you still wear in certain situations?

_____

_____

What would living more authentically look like for you?

_____

_____

Understanding the Impact of Past Experiences on Authenticity

Your identity can become clouded by the expectations, judgments, and narratives imposed by yourself and others. These external influences may lead you to adopt personas that don't reflect your true self as a protective mechanism. Unraveling these layers requires effort but allows you to live authentically. Understanding past experiences is vital, as childhood shapes your self-perception. Supportive interactions can enhance self-worth, while criticism may foster feelings of inadequacy. Recognizing patterns in your behavior and evaluating relationships helps identify those that encourage growth and those that drain your energy, guiding you toward healthier connections and self-discovery.

Activity: Authenticity Blueprint

Your past experiences play a critical role in shaping your sense of self. Supportive interactions can foster self-worth, while criticism can lead to feelings of inadequacy. Acknowledging how these factors influenced your current behaviors is essential for rebuilding your identity.

Core Values Identification

Write down your core values—the principles and beliefs that matter most to you, such as honesty, compassion, adventure, or creativity.

_____

_____

_____

_____

Assessing Authenticity

Identify areas in your life where you feel you are not being your authentic self. This could include work, relationships, or social interactions. Examples might include compromising your values for approval or remaining silent when you wish to speak up.

_____

_____

_____

Action Plan for Authentic Living

Set an action plan for how you can align your daily life more closely with your core values. Consider small, doable steps you can take. For instance, if adventure is a core value, plan a weekend trip or try a new activity you've wanted to explore.

_____

_____

_____

Activity: Support vs. Undermining Relationships

- ❑ **Create two lists**
  - List supportive relationships that nourish your growth.
  - Identify relationships that drain your energy or contribute to feelings of inadequacy.

- ❑ **Reflection questions**
  - How do these supportive relationships enhance your sense of self?
  - What qualities in undermining connections hinder your authentic expression?

_____

_____

_____

Activity: Cultivate Your Tribe

❏ Identify individuals in your life who resonate with your values and aspirations.

❏ Make a plan to reach out to them, share your journey, and discuss how you can support each other in living authentically.

_____

_____

_____

Interactive Exercise: Authenticity Excavation Map

Take a moment to map your journey toward authenticity:

Childhood Influences

❏ Messages received about who to be: _____

❏ When you felt most yourself as a child: _____

❏ When you began hiding parts of yourself: _____

❏ Who encouraged your true self: _____

Current Authenticity Assessment

❏ Situations where I feel most authentic: _____

❏ Situations where I wear masks: _____

❏ Physical sensations of authenticity: _____

❏ Physical sensations of inauthenticity: _____

Authenticity Barriers

❏ Fears about being my true self: _____

❏ External pressures I face: _____

- ❏ Internal narratives holding me back: _____

- ❏ What I need to feel safe being authentic: _____

Authenticity Cultivation

- ❏ Small ways to express my true self: _____

- ❏ People who support my authenticity: _____

- ❏ Boundaries I need to establish: _____

- ❏ Daily practices to strengthen authenticity: _____

Techniques for Personal Introspection and Clarity

Exploring your authentic self through self-reflection is a transformative journey. Let's talk about some helpful techniques.

The Value of Constructive Feedback

Constructive feedback from trusted individuals plays a vital role in highlighting your personal strengths and areas for growth. Sometimes, your self-perception can be clouded by insecurities or overconfidence.

Practical Element

- ❏ **Feedback sessions:** Schedule a feedback session with a respected friend or mentor. Prepare specific questions about your strengths and weaknesses, such as, "What do you think are my greatest strengths?" and "Are there areas you feel I could improve upon?" Take notes during the discussion to reflect on their insights later.

_____

_____

_____

Engaging in Open Conversations

Initiate open conversations with family members, close friends, or mentors who understand your objectives. Share your desire for personal growth and ask for their input on your strengths and weaknesses. Approach these discussions with an open mind and gratitude, acknowledging the courage it takes for someone to provide constructive criticism. Use their feedback not as a definitive assessment but as guidance to refine and strengthen your quest for authenticity.

Practical Element

- ❏ **Check-in Meetings:** Set up regular check-in meetings (monthly or quarterly) with those you trust. Prepare an agenda for these discussions, focusing on what you want to achieve and how they can support you. Be open to feedback and express gratitude for their support.

_____

_____

_____

_____

More Practical Exercises

Explore a variety of engaging exercises designed to reconnect with and nurture your inner child throughout this workbook.

Daily Self-Care Routines and Rituals

Objective

To cultivate confidence and joy through self-care practices.

Instructions

- ❏ Create a list of self-care activities that bring you happiness and fulfillment. Consider aspects such as physical, emotional, and mental well-being (like reading, exercise, meditation).

- ❏ Choose at least three activities from your list to incorporate into your daily routine. Schedule specific times for these activities, ensuring you make them a priority in your day.

❏ Reflect on your experience with these activities over the course of a week. Journal about how they impacted your confidence and emotional state. What feelings arose during or after practicing self-care?

___

___

___

Vision Board Creation

Objective

To visualize and manifest a fulfilled, authentic life through a vision board.

Instructions

❏ Gather materials for a vision board, such as magazines, scissors, glue, markers, and a large piece of poster board.

❏ Take some time to think about your authentic self and what a fulfilling life looks like for you. Consider aspects like personal goals, values, hobbies, relationships, and environments you want to embrace.

❏ Cut out images, words, and phrases that resonate with your vision and arrange them on your poster board. As you create your vision board, focus on how each element reflects your authentic self and aspirations.

❏ Once completed, place your vision board somewhere visible and take a moment to reflect on it daily. Journal about your feelings regarding your vision and any actions you can take to move closer to achieving these goals.

___

___

___

Rediscovering Forgotten Passions

Objective

To cultivate new passions and revive forgotten interests.

Instructions

- ❏ Begin by brainstorming activities or hobbies that brought you joy in the past but may have been neglected over time. Write down as many as come to mind.

- ❏ Choose one or two interests to explore this week. Research or gather resources related to these activities—watch tutorials, read about techniques, or join local groups.

- ❏ Set aside dedicated time this week to engage in these activities. Focus on the process rather than the outcome; immerse yourself in the enjoyment of rediscovering what you love.

- ❏ After each session, journal about your experience. What emotions surfaced? Did practicing this passion ignite any new interests? Reflect on how these activities connect you to your authentic self.

_____

_____

_____

_____

Mindfulness and Reflection Practice

Objective

To enhance self-awareness and emotional clarity through mindfulness.

Instructions

- ❏ Select a quiet space where you can practice mindfulness or meditation. Spend 5–10 minutes focusing on your breath, allowing your thoughts to come and go without judgment.

- ❏ After your mindfulness session, write down any thoughts or emotions that surfaced during your practice. What insights did you gain about your authentic self?

- ❏ Consider incorporating mindfulness into daily activities, such as eating or walking. Write down one or two mindfulness goals for the week, focusing on being present and aware in those moments.

❑ At the end of the week, reflect in your journal on how mindfulness has influenced your ability to connect with your authentic self.

_____
_____
_____

Looking Ahead

As you work through these exercises, notice how your connection to your authentic self evolves. In the next chapter, we'll explore cultivating daily practices for self-love and confidence.

Final Reflection

What's your key takeaway from this chapter?

_____
_____

What practice will you start with tomorrow?

_____
_____

Your Personal Notes

Use this space for additional thoughts and insights:

_____
_____
_____
_____
_____

CHAPTER 2:

Cultivating Daily Practices for Self-Love and Confidence

Self-love is not a fleeting act; it's a dedicated journey of caring for your mind, body, and spirit. In this chapter, we will explore the importance of establishing daily practices that nurture your emotional well-being and build lasting confidence. Instead of relying solely on occasional affirmations or sporadic journaling, you'll learn how to design and maintain a structured self-care routine that supports long-term change and growth.

Quick Check-In Exercise

Before we explore self-love practices, take a moment to check in with yourself:

Rate your current level (1–10):

- ❑ Self-love practice: _____
- ❑ Confidence in daily life: _____
- ❑ Consistency with self-care: _____

What makes you feel most loved by yourself?

_____

_____

What gets in the way of your self-care routine?

_____

_____

What would help you be more consistent with self-love practices?

_____

_____

Designing Personalized Self-Care Routines

Every person's needs are unique, and discovering what truly nurtures you is the first step in your self-love journey. To design a self-care routine, reflect on activities that help you feel energized and balanced. Once you have identified your needs, creating a structured self-care schedule becomes essential.

This schedule acts as a road map, guiding you to prioritize self-care activities and ensuring they don't fall by the wayside in the hustle of daily life. Scheduling specific times for practices like meditation or a walk in nature establishes accountability and reinforces their importance in your daily routine.

Think of this schedule as a commitment to yourself—a promise to nurture your well-being and cultivate a sense of balance. It's beneficial to start small, perhaps dedicating just 10 minutes a day, and then gradually expanding as you become more attuned to the positive impact these practices have on your life.

Positive Affirmation

"I honor my unique needs and prioritize my well-being."

Action Step

List activities that bring you joy (like yoga, drawing, reading) and create a routine that incorporates at least one of these daily.

_____

_____

_____

Creating a Structured Self-Care Schedule

A structured self-care schedule is essential for long-term change. Without a framework, self-care can easily slip to the bottom of your to-do list.

Positive Affirmation

"I dedicate time for self-care as an essential part of my day."

Action Step

Identify specific times each day for self-care—morning, lunch break, or evening—and block those times on your calendar.

_____

_____

_____

This approach transforms self-care from indulgence into an unwavering commitment. By allocating dedicated time, you signal that your well-being is a top priority.

Introducing the Five-Minute Self-Love Ritual

Finding time in a packed day can be challenging. The Five-Minute Self-Love Ritual is a simple, repeatable practice you can easily incorporate into your daily routine.

Step-by-Step Guide

- ❏ **Find a quiet space:** Select a comfortable spot where you won't be disturbed.

- ❏ **Set a timer:** Set a timer for five minutes.

- ❏ **Begin with breath (one minute):** Close your eyes, inhale through your nose, and exhale slowly through your mouth, focusing on your breath.

- ❏ **Conduct a mindful check-in (two minutes):** Scan your body and ask, "How am I feeling?"

- ❏ **Recite a personal statement (one minute):** Choose a positive phrase (like "I am enough") and repeat it.

- ❏ **End with gratitude (one minute):** Acknowledge something about yourself you're grateful for.

- ❏ **Positive affirmation:** Do another positive statement, "I deserve five minutes of love and care every day."

❑ **Action step:** Commit to practicing this self-love ritual daily for a week and note how it makes you feel.

_____
_____
_____

Integrating Mindful Moments Into Daily Life

While the 5-Minute Ritual offers a designated period for self-love, mindfulness can be interwoven into everyday tasks.

Positive Affirmation

"I find joy in the small moments of my day."

Action Step

Identify simple activities (like drinking tea or taking a walk) where you can practice mindfulness. Focus on sensations and create moments of awareness throughout your day.

_____
_____
_____

Interactive Exercise: Self-Love Practice Builder

Take a moment to design your ideal self-love practice:

Morning Rituals

❑ First thoughts upon waking: _____
❑ Physical practices to start your day: _____
❑ Emotional check-in process: _____
❑ Affirmations that resonate: _____

Midday Reconnection

- ❑ Quick grounding techniques: _____
- ❑ Body awareness practices: _____
- ❑ Energy renewal strategies: _____
- ❑ Boundary reinforcement: _____

Evening Reflection

- ❑ Day-release rituals: _____
- ❑ Gratitude focus: _____
- ❑ Self-acknowledgment practice: _____
- ❑ Preparation for restful sleep: _____

Weekly Integration

- ❑ Deeper practices for days off: _____
- ❑ Community or shared experiences: _____
- ❑ Nature connection practices: _____
- ❑ Creative self-expression: _____

Evaluating and Adapting Your Self-Care Practices

The journey to self-love is evolving. Regular evaluations help ensure you're nurturing yourself in effective ways.

Positive Affirmation

"I am open to change and growth in my self-care journey."

Action Step

Reflect on your self-care activities weekly. Are they still energizing and fulfilling? Adjust or replace any practices that no longer resonate with your current needs.

_____

_____

By remaining flexible and continuously aligning your routines with your evolving self, you create a supportive system for long-term well-being.

Building Confidence Through Positive, Personalized Practices

Affirmations are vital in self-love, but daily habits and practices also contribute to your self-worth.

Positive Affirmation

"I celebrate my progress and honor my journey."

Action Step

After your Five-Minute Ritual, take a moment to notice any shifts in your mood or confidence. Journal about how your structured routine enhances your self-esteem.

_____

_____

As you refine your routine, consider sharing your journey with a friend or community. Outside reflections can provide new insights and validate your progress.

The 30-Day Self-Love Tracker

To measure your growth, use the 30-Day Self-Love Tracker. This tool encourages daily accountability and helps you recognize the effects of your self-care practices.

Template

Date: _____

Today's Self-Care Activity:

_____

(Example: Five-Minute Self-Love Ritual, mindful tea break, brisk outdoor walk, or anything you like to engage in.)

1) How did I feel before starting this activity?

2) How do I feel after completing the activity?

3) What did I notice or learn about myself today?

4) What adjustments or new insights can I apply tomorrow

___

Fill out this tracker daily to visualize your progress. Celebrate each change, reinforcing your commitment to self-love.

Flexibility and Adaptability in Your Self-Care Journey

Self-care can sometimes feel confining with a rigid routine. Embrace flexibility to sustain long-term growth.

Positive Affirmation

"I adapt my self-care practices to align with my evolving needs."

Action Step

If a busy day disrupts your routine, engage in a mini version of your ritual. Use that flexibility to reconnect with your emotional and physical needs.

___

Remember: self-love is about progress, not perfection. Each adaptation reinforces your commitment to care, learn, and grow.

More Practical Exercises

Explore a variety of engaging exercises designed to reconnect with and nurture your inner child throughout this workbook.

Designing Your Self-Care Routine

Objective

To create a self-care routine tailored to your individual needs.

Instructions

- ❏ Begin by reflecting on activities that nurture your emotional and physical well-being. Write down at least five activities that resonate with you (e.g., yoga, journaling, nature walks, creative hobbies).

- ❏ Choose three activities from your list to integrate into your daily life. For each chosen activity, write down:
    - Why it is meaningful to you.
    - The specific time you will dedicate to this practice each day or week.

- ❏ Create a self-care schedule for the upcoming week, ensuring you allocate time for each selected activity. Acknowledge this schedule as a commitment to prioritizing your self-care.

_____

_____

_____

_____

Mindfulness Integration Practice

Objective

To enhance self-awareness through mindful moments.

Instructions

- ❏ Identify two daily activities you perform regularly (e.g., drinking coffee, commuting, or brushing your teeth).
- ❏ Set a mindful intention for each activity. For example, while drinking coffee, you might focus on the aroma and taste, appreciating the moment.

- ❏ Practice mindfulness during these activities for one week. After each session, journal about your experience. What thoughts or feelings arose? Did you notice a difference in your emotional state or awareness?

Affirmation Crafting and Implementation

Objective

To develop positive affirmations to boost self-love and confidence.

Instructions

- ❏ Write down five beliefs you would like to change or reinforce in your life (e.g., "I am not good enough" or "I am confident in social situations").

- ❏ For each belief, craft a positive affirmation that counters it, making sure to personalize them. For instance, change "I am not good enough" to "I am worthy and capable of achieving my goals."

- ❏ Choose a specific time each day (morning or evening) to recite your affirmations aloud or silently. Reflect on how repeating these statements influences your thoughts and emotions throughout the week.

Progress Tracking and Reflection Journal

Objective

To monitor your growth through self-care and affirmation practices.

Instructions

- ❏ Throughout the week, maintain a journal to track your experiences with self-care routines and affirmations. For each day, include:

- Self-care activities you engaged in and how they made you feel.
- Any shifts in your mindset related to your affirmations (like increased confidence, reduced anxiety).

❑ At the end of the week, review your entries. Write a summary reflecting on patterns, insights, and any emotional changes you observed. Consider how these practices have impacted your self-love journey.

_____

_____

_____

_____

Flexibility and Adaptation Exercise

Objective

To cultivate a flexible approach to self-care and personal growth.

Instructions

❑ Reflect on a time when you felt overwhelmed by rigid routines or demands. Write about how this rigidity affected your emotional state.

❑ Create a "Flexibility Plan" for your self-care routine. List ways you can allow spontaneity, such as mixing up activities, adjusting the duration based on your mood, or trying new experiences without pressure.

❑ Commit to adapting your self-care practices throughout the next month based on your evolving needs and unexpected life situations. Journal about your experience with these adjustments and how they contribute to your self-love journey.

Looking Ahead

As you work through these exercises, notice how your relationship with yourself evolves through consistent self-love practices. In the next chapter, we'll explore embracing joy and playfulness in everyday life.

Final Reflection

What's your key takeaway from this chapter?

_____

_____

What practice will you start with tomorrow?

_____

_____

Your Personal Notes

Use this space for additional thoughts and insights:

_____

_____

_____

_____

_____

_____

_____

_____

CHAPTER 3:

Embracing Joy and Playfulness in Everyday Life

Embracing joy and playfulness in everyday life is a life-shaping journey that invites us to see the world with fresh eyes and an open heart. This chapter explores the art of integrating these uplifting elements into our daily routines, offering a path to a more fulfilling existence. By learning to incorporate joy and play, individuals can experience a profound shift in how they perceive their surroundings and interact with the world around them. It's not about grand gestures or monumental changes; instead, it's about finding delight in the small moments, which can ultimately lead to sustained happiness and peace.

This chapter discovers various practices designed to blend joy and playfulness seamlessly into everyday activities.

Quick Check-In Exercise

Before we explore joy and playfulness, take a moment to check in with yourself:

Rate your current level (1–10):

- ❑ Joy in daily life: _____
- ❑ Playfulness with yourself and others: _____
- ❑ Spontaneity in your routine: _____

When did you last feel truly joyful?

_____

_____

What activities make you feel most playful?

_____

_____

What activities make you feel most playful?

_____

_____

What prevents you from experiencing more joy?

_____

_____

Practices for Fostering Spontaneous Joy

Inviting joy into your everyday life can often mean shaking up your routines and embracing spontaneous activities. In a world where your schedule is packed and predictability reigns, spontaneity can be the key to reinvigorating your joy. Think of it as an open invitation to explore life's unplanned moments. Taking an unexpected detour on a routine walk, dancing in the rain, or simply allowing yourself a moment of laughter during a busy day can infuse new energy into your life. These small decisions not only break the monotony but also create pockets of happiness that remind you why life is worth celebrating.

A Mindset Shift

The journey to living joyfully involves a mindset shift—one that lets go of rigid plans and embraces the unexpected with open arms. Doing so, you become more attuned to life's nuances and begin to notice opportunities for joy that you might otherwise overlook. Spontaneity fuels your vibrant spirit and encourages a deeper connection with the present moment, making your ordinary days feel extraordinary.

Positive Affirmation

"I welcome spontaneity into my life and embrace the joy of the unexpected."

Practical Exercise: Spontaneity Journal

Instructions

- ❑ **Set an Intention:** At the beginning of the week, set an intention to cultivate spontaneity. Write down a few ideas or activities you've been hesitant to try but feel excited about.
- ❑ **Daily Check-In:** Each day, reflect for a moment on potential opportunities for spontaneous joy. Consider unusual paths you could take during your walk, new dishes to try, or activities you could join at the last minute.
- ❑ **Record Moment:** Whenever you engage in a spontaneous activity, jot it down in your Spontaneity Journal. What did you do? How did it feel? What emotions did it evoke?
- ❑ **Weekly Reflection:** At the end of the week, review your entries. Reflect on how embracing spontaneous moments has impacted your mood and overall sense of joy.

Practicing these techniques, you'll begin to shift your mindset, making space for joy and spontaneity in your life. Each spontaneous decision further deepens your connection to the present, enriching your daily experience with surprises and laughter.

Embracing a Childlike Perspective

Transitioning from spontaneity to a childlike perspective can further amplify your joy. You navigate the world with fresh eyes, eager for discovery and filled with endless curiosity. It's a reminder of the boundless wonder all around you. When you approach life like a child, even mundane tasks transform into adventures waiting to unfold. Washing dishes becomes a sensory experience with bubbles and soapy water; a simple walk outside turns into a mini-exploration of nature's intricacies. Encouraging your curiosity not only renews your appreciation for life's little wonders but invites joy through newfound discoveries.

Positive Affirmation

"I embrace the world with childlike curiosity and wonder."

Practical Exercise: Daily Adventure Challenge

Instructions

- ❑ **Choose an activity:** Select one everyday task that you usually find mundane (e.g., grocery shopping, cleaning, or commuting).

- ❑ **Set an intention for exploration:** Approach this task with the mindset of a child. Before starting, take a moment to set an intention to notice something new or interesting about the activity.

- ❑ **Engage your senses:** While performing the task, consciously engage your senses:

  - What do you see that you might usually overlook?
  - What do you see that you might usually overlook?
  - What sounds fill the space around you?
  - How does the activity feel physically (for example, texture, temperature)?

- ❑ **Document your experience:** After completing the task, take a moment to write about your experience in a journal. What new discoveries did you make? How did approaching the task with curiosity change your perspective?

By incorporating this exercise into your daily life, you'll start to cultivate a childlike sense of wonder, making even ordinary moments feel extraordinary.

Cultivating Curiosity

To develop this mindset, give yourself permission to ask questions about everything you encounter. Challenge preconceived notions and see the beauty in simplicity. Each new perspective has the potential to rekindle your joy, reminding you of how much there is yet to uncover. Joy isn't hidden in grand experiences alone; it's interwoven in daily interactions, revealed when you take a moment to view them through a child's lens.

Positive Affirmation

"I embrace curiosity and open myself to new discoveries every day."

Practical Exercise: Curiosity Quest

Instructions

- ❑ **Select a day:** Choose a specific day this week to dedicate to curiosity. Make it an "Adventure Day."

- ❑ **Create a curiosity list:** Write down three or four everyday activities you will engage in, such as:

- grocery shopping
- commuting to work
- making dinner
- taking a walk

❑ **Ask questions:** As you engage in each task, prepare a list of questions to guide your exploration. For instance:

- What new item can I discover in the grocery store today?
- What interesting details do I notice during my commute?
- How many different colors and textures can I find on my walk?

❑ Document your discoveries: Throughout your day, take notes in a small notebook or your phone about what you learn or notice during these activities. Reflect on how these small discoveries make you feel.

Actively participating in this Curiosity Quest, you'll develop a sense of wonder and appreciation for the world around you. It creates openings for joy in the simplest moments and reminds you that every day holds new potential.

The Practice of Joy Journaling

As these perspective shifts take root, joy journaling can serve as an anchor. A dedicated space where you chronicle positive experiences becomes a repository of happiness—a tangible collection of moments that uplift and inspire. Journaling offers clarity, helping you identify patterns and recognize what brings you joy. Writing down your daily joys shifts your focus away from negativity and fosters gratitude, nurturing a cycle of positive thinking that sharpens your awareness of life's beautiful intricacies.

To begin your joy journaling practice, set aside a quiet moment each day to reflect on events, no matter how small, that sparked your joy. Capture the feelings, sounds, and colors of those instances. Over time, your journal will serve as a testament to the positivity inherent in your life and provide solace during less joyful times. It tangibly represents achieved shifts toward an increasingly joy-focused existence.

Positive Affirmation

"I embrace joy in my life and celebrate the moments that uplift me."

Practical Exercise: Daily Joy Journaling Routine

Instructions

- ❏ **Choose your journal:** Select a journal or digital platform that feels comfortable for you to use regularly.
- ❏ **Set a daily time:** Dedicate a specific time each day—ideally the same time—to reflect on and write about the joyful moments you've experienced. This could be in the morning to set a positive tone for the day or in the evening to reflect on the day's highlights.
- ❏ **Capture highlights:** Each day, write down at least three things that brought you joy, no matter how small. Describe the feelings, sounds, and colors associated with each moment to enrich your entries.
- ❏ **Example:** "Today, the warm sun on my face during my walk brought me joy. I could hear the birds singing, and the flowers were blooming in vibrant colors."
- ❏ **Review weekly:** At the end of each week, take some time to read back through your entries. Note any recurring themes or activities that brought you joy, and consider how you can incorporate more of these into your life.

The Power of Kindness

Engaging in acts of kindness can be a powerful conduit for experiencing joy. Helping others creates ripples of positivity—both for you as the giver and for the receiver. These connections foster a sense of belonging that nurtures joy within communities and individuals alike. Whether offering a listening ear, volunteering your time, or extending a kind gesture, reaching out builds bonds and highlights our shared humanity.

Positive Affirmation

"I spread joy through acts of kindness, and in doing so, I enrich my own life."

Practical Exercise: Kindness Challenge

Instructions

- ❏ **Set a timeframe:** Choose a week to dedicate to acts of kindness. This could be any seven-day period that works for you.
- ❏ **Identify kind acts:** Write down five specific acts of kindness you can perform during this week. These can range from simple gestures to more involved actions. Examples include:

a) complimenting a coworker.

b) sending a thoughtful message to a friend.

c) volunteering at a local charity.

d) helping a neighbor with groceries.

e) donating to a cause you care about.

- ❑ **Execute your kind acts:** Carry out these acts of kindness throughout the week, aiming to complete at least one each day.

- ❑ **Reflect on your experience:** After the week, spend a few moments journaling about how engaging in these acts made you feel. Did you notice a shift in your mood? How did the recipients respond? Consider how these acts of kindness impacted your sense of joy.

Discovering joy through service, purpose emerges, bringing fulfillment that goes beyond personal happiness. Kindness creates a mutual exchange of joy, reinforcing the belief that everyone shares in the rewards of giving. To practice this, consider where your passions and skills align with community needs. Engage with causes that resonate deeply, and relish in the collective empowerment realized through every contribution made.

Interactive Exercise: Joy Map Creation

Take a moment to map the landscape of joy in your life:

Joy Inventory

❑ Activities that consistently bring joy: _____

❑ People who spark joy in your life: _____

❑ Places where you feel most joyful: _____

❑ Simple pleasures you treasure: _____

Playfulness Exploration

❑ Childhood games you loved: _____

- ❏ Ways you could be more playful today: _____
- ❏ Playful activities you'd like to try: _____
- ❏ How you express playfulness now: _____

Joy Barriers

- ❏ What stops you from being playful: _____
- ❏ Self-judgment that limits joy: _____
- ❏ External pressures against playfulness: _____
- ❏ How you can overcome these barriers: _____

Joy Integration Plan

- ❏ Morning joy infusion: _____
- ❏ Midday playfulness break: _____
- ❏ Evening joy ritual: _____
- ❏ Weekly play date with yourself: _____

Incorporating Playfulness Into Routines

Embracing joy and playfulness in your everyday life is more than just a nice-to-have addition; it's a life-changing journey toward enhanced well-being and fulfillment. Understanding how to integrate play into your daily routines can impact your life. At the forefront of this transformation is cultivating a playful mindset, which has myriad benefits. This mindset encourages creativity and flexibility. When you approach tasks with a sense of play, you're more likely to think outside the box and develop innovative solutions. This creativity is satisfying and reduces stress, making even the most mundane activities enjoyable.

Problem-Solving and Creativity

The satisfaction that comes from solving problems creatively fosters a positive feedback loop for you. As you become more open-minded, you find yourself adapting to changes with greater ease, enhancing your overall satisfaction with life. A playful mindset allows you to see challenges as opportunities rather than obstacles. This shift in perspective can make a world of difference in how you experience stress and joy daily.

Gamifying Daily Tasks

Gamifying daily tasks can also enhance your motivation and productivity. By turning routines into fun challenges, you inject a sense of excitement into otherwise tedious activities. Applying gamification principles involves setting specific goals, tracking progress, and rewarding achievements.

For instance, changing a boring task like cleaning into a timed race against yourself or others can boost your motivation. Friendly competitions, whether with yourself or friends, add an element of fun that keeps things interesting. These playful competitions encourage you to strive for better performance, elevating your productivity and engagement.

Guidelines: To gamify tasks effectively, identify repetitive actions that you can quantify or measure. Set achievable milestones and celebrate each success, no matter how small. Use apps or simple paper trackers to visualize your progress—a technique commonly employed in video games to maintain player interest. This visual feedback heightens your awareness of development and provides additional satisfaction.

Incorporating Movement

Physical movement is another avenue through which you can bring playfulness into your everyday life. Finding joy in movement by incorporating dance or playful stretching into your activities can raise your mood substantially. The connection between physical activity and improved mental health is well-documented. Engaging in joyful movements releases endorphins, those feel-good hormones that help diminish stress and anxiety. Dancing around the kitchen while cooking or taking short breaks to stretch playfully at your workstation are easy ways for you to introduce joy into your routine. These lighthearted activities relieve tension and infuse your daily life with happiness, encouraging a habit of moving joyfully.

Guidelines: Identify moments in your day where movement can be naturally integrated. It may be during breaks from work or as part of your morning or evening routines. Listen to your favorite upbeat music or challenge yourself to learn new dance steps online for added fun and excitement.

Establishing Lighthearted Rituals

Finally, establishing lighthearted rituals that incorporate humor can deepen your relationships and create lasting memories. Sharing laughter strengthens bonds with friends and family, fostering a supportive community atmosphere. Humor has a way of breaking down barriers and allowing genuine connections to form. Consider starting your day with a funny video or joke-sharing session at breakfast to set a positive tone for the day ahead. These small yet impactful rituals build a reserve of joyful memories that you can draw upon during difficult times, providing comfort and maintaining positivity.

Guideline: To create these rituals, involve others in the process. Collaborate on ideas and set aside specific times to engage in these activities. Whether it's a weekly game night with friends or a silly tradition like "Wear Your Wackiest Socks Day" at home, the key is consistency and shared participation.

More Practical Exercises

Explore a variety of engaging exercises designed to reconnect with and nurture your inner child throughout this workbook.

Spontaneous Joy Exploration

Objective

To invite joy into your life through spontaneous activities.

Instructions

- ❑ Reflect on your daily routine and identify areas where you can introduce spontaneity. Write down three opportunities (e.g., taking a different route while walking, trying a new café, or attempting a spontaneous dance break).

- ❑ Choose one spontaneous activity to incorporate into your week. Plan a specific time for this activity, and allow yourself to embrace the unexpected with joy.

- ❑ After the experience, journal about how it made you feel. Did it spark joy? How did it change your perspective on your daily routine?

_____

_____

_____

Childlike Perspective Practice

Objective

To cultivate curiosity and joy by adopting a childlike perspective.

Instructions

- ❏ Spend a day or two observing your environment as if you were a child. Write down three ordinary activities you typically overlook (e.g., walking in your neighborhood, cooking, or cleaning).
- ❏ For each activity, create a list of questions you might ask a child about it (e.g., What do you notice? How does this feel? What colors do you see?).
- ❏ Engage in these activities with your newfound curiosity, allowing yourself to explore and wonder about the ordinary. Journal your observations and feelings afterward, focusing on any joy or discoveries you encountered.

_____

_____

_____

Joy Journaling Habit

Objective

To create a habit of recognizing and documenting moments of joy.

Instructions

- ❏ Set aside 5–10 minutes each day to reflect on and write down three things that brought you joy, no matter how small. These can include feelings, sights, sounds, or interactions.
- ❏ Consider establishing a dedicated journal or app for this purpose. Decorate your journal cover to make it inviting and special.
- ❏ At the end of the week, look back at your entries. Write a summary of the patterns you observe and how focusing on joy has impacted your mood and outlook.

_____

_____

Acts of Kindness to Encourage Joy

Objective

To bring joy to others and yourself through acts of kindness.

Instructions

- ❑ Reflect on your community and identify three ways you can extend kindness to others (e.g., volunteering, helping a neighbor, or sending a thoughtful note).
- ❑ Choose one act of kindness to commit to in the upcoming week. Write down the details and plan when you will carry it out.
- ❑ After completing the act, journal about the experience. How did it affect your mood? What feelings did it evoke, both in you and the recipient?

_____

_____

_____

Gamifying Daily Tasks

Objective

To increase motivation and joy through playful challenges.

Instructions

- ❑ Identify three routine tasks in your life that feel mundane (like cleaning your room, doing the dishes, or exercising).
- ❑ Create a game by setting specific goals or challenges for each task. For example, challenge yourself to complete the dishes in under ten minutes or turn cleaning into a dance party with your favorite playlist.
- ❑ Track your progress and celebrate each completed challenge. Reflect on how gamifying these tasks affected your willingness to engage with them and your overall mood.

_____

_____

_____

Looking Ahead

As you work through these exercises, notice how joy and playfulness transform your daily experience. In the next chapter, we'll explore sustaining inner peace through personal growth.

Final Reflection

What's your key takeaway from this chapter?

_____

_____

What practice will you start with tomorrow?

_____

_____

Your Personal Notes

Use this space for additional thoughts and insights:

_____

_____

_____

_____

_____

_____

_____

CHAPTER 4:

Sustaining Inner Peace Through Personal Growth

Welcome to your journey of sustaining inner peace through personal growth. In this chapter, we'll explore practical tools and exercises that help you create lasting emotional stability in an often chaotic world. Think of this chapter as your personal guide to building a sanctuary of calm within yourself—not through complex rituals, but through simple, consistent practices that yield profound results.

Quick Check-In Exercise

Take a moment to reflect on your current relationship with inner peace:

_____

_____

Rate your current level of inner peace (1–10): _____

What disrupts your peace most often?

_____

_____

What currently helps you feel peaceful?

_____

_____

Understanding Inner Peace and Personal Growth

Before we dive into the practical exercises, let's understand what we mean by inner peace. It's not about eliminating all stress or negative emotions from your life—that's neither realistic nor helpful. Instead, it's about developing the ability to maintain emotional balance and clarity, even when facing life's challenges. This journey combines mindfulness practices with personal development strategies, creating a foundation for lasting tranquility.

Mindfulness Exercises for Emotional Balance

Mindfulness serves as our anchor in maintaining emotional equilibrium. Let's explore practical exercises that you can integrate into your daily life, starting with the basics and building up to more advanced practices.

Beginning Mindfulness Meditation

Start Here Exercise:

1) Find a quiet spot where you won't be interrupted

2) Set a timer for five minutes

3) Sit comfortably, either on a chair or cushion

4) Focus on your breath moving in and out

5) When your mind wanders (it will!), gently return to your breath

Daily Practice Log

Date	Duration	Focus used	How did it feel

Body Scan Meditation

A body scan helps you develop awareness of physical sensations and release tension.

Practice Steps

1) Lie down comfortably on your back

2) Close your eyes and take three deep breaths

3) Begin at your toes, moving attention slowly up through your body

4) Notice any sensations without trying to change them

5) Spend 15–30 seconds on each body part

6) If you notice tension, breathe into that area and let it soften

Body Scan Log

Date	Areas of tension	Insights gained	After effects

Mindful Walking Practice

Transform a regular walk into a mindfulness exercise.

Instructions

1) Choose a quiet path or space

2) Walk at a slower pace than usual

3) Notice the sensation of each foot lifting and placing

4) Feel the movement of your legs and arms

5) Observe your surroundings with full attention

6) When your mind wanders, return to the physical sensations of walking

Practice Record

Location	Duration	What I noticed	How I felt after

Sound Awareness Meditation

This practice helps sharpen your present-moment awareness using sounds.

Steps

1) Sit or lie comfortably

2) Close your eyes

3) Listen to the sounds around you without labeling them

4) Notice near and far sounds

5) Pay attention to the quality of each sound

6) Notice the spaces between sounds

Sound Mapping Exercise

Draw or write the sounds you hear in these concentric circles:

[Create three concentric circles on the page]

Closest to me:

DRAW OR WRITE THE SOUNDS YOU HEAR

Middle distance:

_____

Far away:

_____

Loving-Kindness Practice

This meditation cultivates compassion for yourself and others.

Basic Practice:

☐ Start with yourself, then expand to:
- a loved one
- a neutral person
- a difficult person
- all beings

Phrases to Use:

☐ May I/you be happy
☐ May I/you be healthy
☐ May I/you be safe
☐ May I/you live with ease

Daily Practice Log

Who	Phrases used	Feelings arose	Insights
Self			
Loved one			
Neutral person			
Difficult person			

Breathing Techniques for Immediate Calm

Practice these two powerful breathing exercises:

Box Breathing

1) Inhale for 4 counts
2) Hold for 4 counts
3) Exhale for 4 counts
4) Hold for 4 counts
5) Repeat 4 times

Diaphragmatic Breathing

1) Place one hand on your chest and one on your belly
2) Breathe so your belly expands more than your chest
3) Exhale slowly through pursed lips
4) Practice for 5 breaths

Track Your Practice

When did you use these techniques today?

- ❏ Morning: _____
- ❏ Afternoon: _____
- ❏ Evening: _____

Grounding Techniques

Use this 5-4-3-2-1 exercise when feeling overwhelmed:

List:

- ❏ 5 things you can see: _____
- ❏ 4 things you can touch: _____
- ❏ 3 things you can hear: _____
- ❏ 2 things you can smell: _____
- ❏ 1 thing you can taste: _____

Gratitude and Reflection Practice

Daily Gratitude Journal

Today I'm grateful for:

1) _____

2) _____

3) _____

Why these matter to me:

_____

_____

_____

Interactive Exercise: Personal Peace Ecosystem

Take a moment to map your personal peace ecosystem:

Peace Contributors

- ❑ Activities that restore my peace: _____
- ❑ People who support my calm: _____
- ❑ Environments where I feel centered: _____
- ❑ Thoughts that bring tranquility: _____

Peace Disruptors

- ❑ Common stressors in my life: _____
- ❑ Relationship dynamics that create tension: _____
- ❑ Environmental factors that agitate me: _____
- ❑ Thought patterns that disturb peace: _____

Peace Protection Plan

- ❑ Early warning signs of peace disruption: _____
- ❑ Immediate actions when feeling unbalanced: _____
- ❑ Boundaries I need to establish: _____
- ❑ Communication phrases for maintaining peace: _____

Peace Restoration Practices

- ❑ Quick reset techniques (under 5 minutes): _____
- ❑ Medium practices (15–30 minutes): _____
- ❑ Deep restoration practices (over 30 minutes): _____
- ❑ Resources to access when needed: _____

Growth Strategies for Resilience and Peace

In a world where chaos often reigns, maintaining inner peace is essential. Building resilience is crucial for navigating life's challenges while fostering personal growth. One of the foundational steps in this journey is identifying core values. These values serve as an internal compass, guiding decisions and actions through turbulent times. When you know what's truly important to you—whether it's honesty, compassion, or creativity—you can stand firm in your beliefs, finding solace even amidst uncertainty.

Developing resilience is crucial for maintaining inner peace. Let's explore practical ways to build this essential quality.

Identifying Your Core Values

Pinpointing your core values requires introspection. Take time to reflect on moments when you felt truly fulfilled or deeply upset; these emotions often signal where your values lie. Once identified, integrate them into your daily life by using them as criteria for decision-making. This alignment provides consistency, which promotes authenticity and reduces inner conflict. When life throws curveballs, returning to your core values offers a grounding force—a reminder of what truly matters and a pathway back to peace.

Values Clarification Exercise

Identify your top five core values:

1) _____

2) _____

3) _____

4) _____

5) _____

How do these values guide your decisions?

_____

_____

_____

_____

Communicating Your Needs

Communicate clearly and assertively with those around you. Express what behaviors you find acceptable and which ones you don't. For example, if work encroaches on your personal time, practice asserting your needs by setting specific work hours. By doing so, you're protecting yourself and teaching others how to treat you. The result is less stress, improved relationships, and increased resilience—all critical for sustaining your inner peace.

Cultivating a Growth Mindset

Resilience also flourishes when you cultivate a growth mindset. Embracing a growth mindset means viewing challenges as opportunities rather than insurmountable obstacles. It involves understanding that abilities can be developed through dedication and effort. With this approach, failures transform from devastating blows into invaluable learning experiences.

Self-Compassion Practice

When facing difficulties, complete this self-compassion note:

Dear self,

_____

_____

_____

_____

_____

Setbacks as Stepping Stones

Begin to develop a growth mindset by reframing your setbacks. Instead of seeing failure as a reflection of inadequacy, view it as a stepping stone toward mastery. Acknowledge your progress, no matter how small, and celebrate effort over results. Stories of renowned innovators like Thomas Edison, who famously saw each failed experiment as a lesson learned, serve as inspiration here. Such perspectives fuel perseverance, gradually bolstering your resilience and deepening your sense of peace.

Reframing Challenges Exercise

Think of a current challenge you're facing:

- ❑ Challenge: _____

- ❑ Current thought about it: _____

- ❑ Reframed as an opportunity: _____

- ❑ Possible learning outcomes: _____

Integrating Mindfulness into Daily Life

Now let's create practical ways to weave mindfulness into your everyday routine.

Morning Mindfulness Routine

Design your ideal morning routine:

Time	Activity	Duration

Mindful Moments Throughout the Day

Identify three regular daily activities you can do mindfully:

1) _____

2) _____

3) _____

Evening Wind-Down Practice

Create your peaceful evening routine:

- ❑ First step: _____
- ❑ Second step: _____
- ❑ Final step: _____

Action Steps for Lasting Peace

In the pursuit of lasting peace, embracing actionable steps is essential for promoting harmony and understanding in your life and community.

Vision Board Planning

If you haven't created your visual board yet, this is another opportunity to start.

Materials needed:

- ❏ large board or paper
- ❏ magazines/images
- ❏ scissors
- ❏ glue
- ❏ markers

Areas to include:

- ❏ Personal growth goals: _____
- ❏ Emotional well-being: _____
- ❏ Relationships: _____
- ❏ Career/Purpose: _____
- ❏ Health/Self-care: _____

Weekly Peace Practice Planner

The Weekly Peace Practice Planner is designed to help you cultivate mindfulness and tranquility in your daily routine, providing a structured approach to nurturing your inner peace.

Day	Morning practice	Afternoon check-in	Evening routine

Monthly Progress Reflection

Set aside time each month to review your journey:

Review Questions:

❑ What new practices worked best? _____

❑ What challenges did I overcome? _____

❑ How has my inner peace grown? _____

❑ What needs adjustment? _____

Practical Tips for Maintaining Your Practice

1) **Start small:** Begin with five-minute practices and gradually increase duration

2) **Be consistent:** Choose a regular time for your practices

3) **Create triggers:** Link new practices to existing habits

4) **Track progress:** Use the provided logs and journals

5) **Stay flexible:** Adjust practices as needed to fit your life

Remember:

❑ Inner peace is a journey, not a destination

❑ Small, consistent steps lead to significant change

❑ It's okay to have days when peace feels distant

❑ Return to these exercises whenever needed

More Practical Exercises

Explore a variety of engaging exercises designed to reconnect with and nurture your inner child throughout this workbook.

Daily Rituals

Creating daily self-care routines can enhance your sense of confidence and joy. Take a moment each day to prioritize your well-being. Here's a simple structure to create your personalized self-care routine:

- ❑ **Morning ritual:** Start your day with intention. Write down three things you're grateful for as soon as you wake up. Follow this with a five-minute mindfulness meditation focusing on your breath.
- ❑ **Midday break:** Dedicate a short time during your day, perhaps during lunch, to step outside and connect with nature. Observe your surroundings and take five deep breaths to recenter yourself.
- ❑ **Evening reflection:** Before going to bed, journal about your day. What made you feel confident or joyful? What challenges did you face, and how did you overcome them? Reflecting on these moments strengthens your self-awareness.

_____

_____

_____

Discover Old and New Passions

Rediscovering passions and cultivating new interests can foster personal growth. Engage in the following exercises to reconnect with what you love:

- ❑ **Passion inventory:** Write down hobbies or activities you enjoyed in the past that you may have set aside. Reflect on why you loved them and how they made you feel.
- ❑ **New exploration:** Choose one new activity you've always wanted to try; it could be painting, dancing, or learning a musical instrument. Dedicate a specific time each week to engage in this activity without judgment or pressure.
- ❑ **Connect with others:** Join a local class or online group focused on your chosen activity. Meeting new people who share similar interests can reignite your passions and bring new joy into your life.

_____

_____

_____

Looking Ahead

As you work through these exercises, notice how your relationship with inner peace evolves. In the next chapter, we'll explore the ongoing journey to achieving wholeness.

Final Reflection

What's your key takeaway from this chapter?

_____

_____

What practice will you start with tomorrow?

_____

_____

Your Personal Notes

Use this space for additional thoughts and insights:

_____

_____

_____

_____

_____

_____

_____

CHAPTER 5:

Rediscovering Your Authentic Self After Healing

Your ongoing journey to wholeness is a unique and personal pursuit that invites you to reflect deeply on your own goals, dreams, and values. In this chapter, you are guided through practical approaches to goal-setting, using frameworks like SMART criteria to bring structure and clarity to your aspirations.

Quick Check-In Exercise

Before we explore your ongoing journey to wholeness, take a moment to check in with yourself:

Rate your current level (1–10):

- ❑ Clarity about personal definition of success: _____
- ❑ Alignment between goals and values: _____
- ❑ Connection with supportive community: _____

What does "wholeness" mean to you personally?

_____

_____

What parts of yourself are you still learning to integrate?

_____

_____

What would your life look like if you felt truly whole?

_____

_____

Setting Long-Term Goals for Personal Well-Being

Obtaining personal wholeness and fulfillment is a lifelong endeavor, enriched by cultivating a long-term vision for one's well-being and development. This process begins with defining personal success in a manner that harmonizes with one's core values and authentic self.

Your Journey to Personal Wholeness and Fulfillment

Obtaining personal wholeness and fulfillment is a lifelong endeavor, enriched by cultivating a long-term vision for your well-being and development. This process begins with defining your personal success in a manner that harmonizes with your core values and authentic self.

Challenging Societal Norms

Traditional societal norms often impose rigid definitions of success based on external accomplishments like wealth or status. However, genuine personal success is deeply personal and unique to you. By introspecting and understanding what truly inspires and fulfills you at a core level, you can challenge these conventional ideas and create a definition of success that resonates with your true self.

Reflecting on Joy and Satisfaction

To facilitate your personal exploration, consider reflecting on what brings you joy and satisfaction in everyday life. Ask yourself questions like: What activities make me lose track of time? When do I feel most alive and true to myself? The answers to these questions can provide insights into your personal goals and values. Embracing this individualized understanding of success allows you to pursue paths aligned with your passions and desires, rather than conforming to external pressures. It becomes a guiding star on your ongoing journey to wholeness, encouraging decisions that foster personal growth and well-being.

Implementing Goal-Setting Frameworks

As your definitions of success are formed, implementing goal-setting frameworks can offer structure and clarity. One practical approach is using the SMART criteria—Specific, Measurable, Achievable, Relevant, and Time-bound. Applying this framework ensures your goals are clear and actionable while allowing for adaptability over time. For example, instead of setting a vague goal, such as "improve my health," a SMART goal would specify "attend yoga classes twice a week for three months." This provides not only motivation but also a tangible measure of progress.

Embracing Continuous Reflection

Goal-setting frameworks encourage continuous reflection and adjustment, accommodating the dynamic nature of personal growth. As you evolve, so too should your goals be reassessed and realigned with your emerging aspirations and values. This adaptive process cultivates resilience and flexibility, essential traits for maintaining momentum on the path to fulfillment.

Utilizing Visualization Techniques

In tandem with structured goal-setting, visualization techniques offer powerful tools for envisioning your desired future. Visualization involves creating vivid mental images of achieving your goals, reinforcing motivation and focus. Studies suggest that imagining yourself accomplishing a task activates similar brain areas as actually completing it, providing psychological reinforcement. Techniques like guided imagery or vision boards can be employed to bolster this practice, making abstract dreams tangible and achievable.

Dedicating Time for Visualization

Consider dedicating a few minutes daily to visualize specific scenarios related to your goals. Imagine the feelings of accomplishment and the sense of satisfaction upon reaching milestones. These mental rehearsals build confidence and instill a sense of purpose, steering you closer to your envisioned futures. Visualization also supports emotional preparedness, equipping you with the mindset needed to overcome obstacles along the way.

Celebrating Your Milestones

Celebrating milestones along your journey is equally important. Acknowledging your achievements, no matter how small, reinforces positive behavior and fosters gratitude. Celebrations need not be extravagant; they can be as simple as sharing your accomplishments with a friend, journaling about your experiences, or treating yourself to a favorite activity. Recognizing progress enhances motivation and resilience, generating a positive feedback loop.

Reflect on past victories and take note of the strengths and skills developed through overcoming challenges. Celebrating these moments cultivates self-compassion, reminding individuals that growth is an incremental process. This practice not only builds confidence but also creates a reservoir of positive memories to draw upon during difficult times, nurturing an enduring sense of gratitude and appreciation for one's journey.

Interactive Exercise: Wholeness Integration Map

Take a moment to map the elements of your wholeness journey:

Personal Success Vision

- ❑ What success means to me: _____
- ❑ How this differs from conventional success: _____
- ❑ Values that guide my definition: _____
- ❑ How I'll know when I've achieved it: _____

Life Purpose Exploration

- ❑ Activities that energize me: _____
- ❑ Skills I most enjoy using: _____
- ❑ Problems I feel drawn to solve: _____
- ❑ Legacy I want to create: _____

Community Constellation

- ❑ People who support my authentic self: _____

- ❏ Communities that nurture my growth: _____
- ❏ Mentors who inspire me: _____
- ❏ How I support others in return: _____

Growth Continuity Plan

- ❏ How I'll maintain momentum: _____
- ❏ Regular check-in practices: _____
- ❏ Resources for ongoing learning: _____
- ❏ How I'll adapt as I evolve: _____

Nurturing Connections with Supportive Communities

In the ongoing journey toward personal wholeness and fulfillment, the role of supportive relationships and communities is pivotal. These connections act as catalysts, encouraging growth by providing a nurturing environment where one can truly thrive.

Building a Tribe

Identifying those who align with your growth goals—your tribe—is the first step. A tribe consists of individuals who resonate with your values and aspirations, providing not only moral support but also practical resources. To identify these people, it's important to engage in environments where like-minded individuals gather. This might be through forums, local meetups, or online groups focused on personal development.

Building meaningful relationships within this tribe requires effort and intentionality. Trust and communication form the backbone of any solid relationship. When trust is established, it creates a safe space for vulnerability, allowing individuals to share their struggles and triumphs without fear of judgment. Consistent and open communication further strengthens these bonds. For example, setting regular check-ins with friends or mentors can help maintain strong connections and ensure mutual support. These relationships positively impact emotional well-being by providing reassurance and validation during times of self-doubt or struggle.

Participating in Structured Group Activities

These activities offer another layer of support and accountability. Joining community activities, workshops, or support groups presents opportunities to bond over shared experiences and challenges. These settings not only provide a platform for learning new skills but also foster a sense of belonging. Engaging with such groups can lead to personal insights and breakthroughs, often facilitated by the diverse perspectives within the group. For instance, a book club centered on personal development literature might inspire members to apply new concepts in their lives, fueling both personal and collective growth.

Developing Supportive Environments

Creating a supportive environment is essential for sustaining these relationships and ensuring they continue to contribute positively to personal growth. While guidelines should not overwhelm, establishing clear intentions for the type of environment you wish to cultivate can be beneficial. This could involve setting boundaries that protect your time and energy, choosing to engage in spaces that encourage positivity and growth, and being deliberate about the influences you allow into your life. For example, curating a social media feed that resonates with your personal goals can enhance positivity and motivation.

Cultivating authenticity within these settings encourages genuine interactions and allows real connections to flourish. When individuals feel free to express their true selves, the interactions become richer and more meaningful. Supportive environments are characterized by empathy, active listening, and willingness to understand differing viewpoints. This type of environment enhances personal fulfillment by allowing individuals to explore various facets of their identity without fear.

Shared Resources

The value of shared resources cannot be understated in this journey. Whether it's exchanging books, attending seminars together, or sharing tools that aid personal growth, having access to diverse resources enriches the experience. The value of these shared resources lies not just in the information they provide but in the bonding that occurs through shared learning experiences. These interactions can spark discussions that deepen understanding and ignite passion for continued growth.

Exercise: Community Connection Mapping

Objective

To identify, evaluate, and strengthen your supportive community connections.

Instructions

Part 1: Map Your Current Community

Draw a circle in the center of a page and write your name in it. Then create three concentric circles around it:

- ❏ Inner circle: People who deeply support your authentic self
- ❏ Middle circle: People who are generally supportive
- ❏ Outer circle: Acquaintances with growth potential

Place names in each circle, considering:

- ❏ Who celebrates your successes?
- ❏ Who offers honest feedback with compassion?
- ❏ Who encourages your personal growth?
- ❏ Who accepts you as you truly are?

Part 2: Quality of Connection Assessment

For each person in your inner and middle circles, reflect on:

Connection name	Authenticity (1–10)	Growth support (1–10)	Mutual exchange (1–10)

Part 3: Community Gaps Analysis

Reflect on what might be missing in your current community:

- ❏ What types of support do you need that you're not getting?
- ❏ What perspectives would enrich your growth journey?
- ❏ What qualities in relationships help you feel most whole?

Missing support	Potential sources	Action steps

Part 4: Connection Nurturing Plan

Choose three relationships you'd like to strengthen:

Relationship	Why it matters	Next connection step	Frequency

Part 5: Group Involvement Strategy

Identify groups or communities that align with your values and growth:

Type of community	What it offers	How to engage	Commitment level

Reflection Questions

- ❑ How do your strongest connections reflect your core values?
- ❑ In what ways has your community supported your personal growth?
- ❑ What boundaries might you need to set within certain relationships?

❏ How can you contribute more meaningfully to your community?

_____

_____

_____

Your journey to wholeness is uniquely individual yet deeply intertwined with the community you cultivate around you. By intentionally seeking out a tribe, investing in meaningful relationships, participating actively in groups, and creating a supportive environment, one builds a foundation that supports continuous personal evolution. Every interaction and connection becomes a stepping stone toward greater emotional resilience and inner peace.

More Practical Exercises

Explore a variety of engaging exercises designed to reconnect with and nurture your inner child throughout this workbook.

Exercise 1: Defining Personal Success

Take a moment to define what success means to you personally. Reflect on your values, passions, and what brings you joy.

1) Write down your definition of success in a few sentences.

2) List at least three activities that make you lose track of time.

3) Identify moments in your life when you felt most fulfilled. What were you doing during those times?

_____

_____

_____

Exercise 2: Goal-Setting With SMART Criteria

Using the SMART framework, create one specific goal that aligns with your newly defined personal success.

What is your starting goal?

_____

1) Make it Specific: What exactly do you want to achieve?

2) Ensure it is Measurable: How will you track your progress?

3) Make it Achievable: Is this goal realistic for you?

4) Ensure it's Relevant: How does this goal align with your values?

5) Make it Time-bound: When do you intend to achieve this goal?

_____

_____

_____

Exercise 3: Visualization Practice

Spend a few minutes practicing visualization for the goal you've set in Exercise 2.

1) Close your eyes and imagine yourself achieving this goal. What do you see, hear, and feel?

2) Write down a detailed description of this vision. Include the emotions you feel and the environment around you.

3) What new opportunities open up for you once you achieve this goal?

_____

_____

_____

Exercise 4: Celebrating Milestones

Celebration is key in acknowledging your progress.

1) List at least five milestones related to your goal.

2) For each milestone, write an enjoyable way to celebrate it once achieved.

3) Commit to celebrating even small victories by establishing a habit of gratitude. Write down one thing you're grateful for each day related to your journey.

_____

_____

_____

Exercise 5: Building Your Supportive Community

Identify your "tribe" and how they can support your journey.

1) List at least three people in your life who support your growth. How do they influence you positively?

2) Consider joining a group, club, or online community that focuses on personal development. Write down any communities you are interested in exploring.

3) Reflect on how you can be a supportive member in your chosen community. What strengths can you offer?

_____

_____

_____

Exercise 6: Reflective Journaling

Finally, take time each week to reflect on your journey.

1) Write about the challenges you faced while pursuing your goals.

2) How did you overcome those challenges?

3) What insights have you gained about yourself?

_____

_____

_____

_____

Remember: Growth is not linear. Honor your journey through both challenges and triumphs, knowing each experience contributes to your authentic wholeness.

Looking Ahead

As you conclude this workbook series, remember that your journey to wholeness is ongoing and ever-evolving. The practices, insights and connections you've developed throughout these workbooks will continue to support your growth long after you've completed the final page.

Final Reflection

What's your key takeaway from this journey?

_____

_____

What will you continue to nurture in yourself?

_____

_____

Your Personal Notes

Use this space for additional thoughts and insights:

_____

_____

_____

_____

_____

_____

_____

CONCLUSION

Discovering your true self, loving yourself, enjoying life, and finding inner peace is personal and different for you. Each step you take shows your strength and commitment to growing.

The lessons you learn and the habits you choose are gifts that improve your life and those around you. Embracing these ideas transforms you and positively affects your relationships and communities. Living genuinely inspires others to embark on their own journeys of self-discovery. Authenticity fosters empathy and trust, leading to honest communication and connections built on acceptance and respect. Your joyful energy encourages creativity and optimism, and by embracing playful moments, you challenge norms and motivate others to pursue their passions.

Through mindfulness, you recognize the interconnectedness of all things and learn to appreciate fleeting moments. This awareness deepens empathy and compassion, making you an advocate for sustainable living and harmony with nature. Mindfulness guides you in making choices aligned with your values, ensuring a better future for coming generations. This journey invites you to reclaim your true self, celebrate joy, and find inner peace.

Personal growth is an ongoing journey requiring curiosity, patience, and kindness to yourself. Every effort contributes to collective healing, and each practice, no matter how small, enriches your story. Reflect on your progress, celebrate achievements, and embrace uncertainty. Trust that authenticity, joy, and peace are within reach. By doing this, you honor your commitment to navigate your journey with determination. May the lessons you learn guide your path, nurturing change and leading to a life of purpose, love, and fulfillment.

FINAL REFLECTIONS

As we conclude this life-changing journey through the *Healing Your Inner Child Workbook 5-in-1* series, it's vital to take a moment and reflect on the insights and learnings that have emerged along the way. Each component of this series has been meticulously designed to provide you with practical tools for emotional healing, self-discovery, and personal growth. Through engaging with these materials, you have gone on an exploration of your inner world—a process that is courageous and deeply rewarding.

Throughout these chapters, we have looked into the complexities of childhood trauma and its long-lasting impact on adult relationships. You have learned how formative experiences shape emotional responses and behavioral patterns, often leading to self-sabotaging habits that can hinder authentic connections. Recognizing these patterns is the first step toward breaking free from them. The insights gained from understanding the links between your past and present serve as critical turning points in your journey, allowing you to confront and heal from old wounds that have shaped your identity.

The emphasis on nurturing your inner child throughout this series has been a cornerstone of your healing process. By reconnecting with the child within you, acknowledging their fears and desires, you have opened doors to self-compassion and acceptance. This process facilitates not just healing but also reconnection with joy, creativity, and a sense of playfulness that may have been overshadowed by life's demands. Embracing your inner child empowers you to reclaim lost aspects of yourself, enhancing your overall well-being.

The series highlights the importance of setting healthy boundaries in relationships. You have explored how boundaries protect your emotional health and promote mutual respect. Communicating your needs assertively and sustaining relationships grounded in trust and authenticity has helped you create a supportive environment for growth. This newfound assertiveness reinforces your self-worth, enabling you to engage more meaningfully with yourself and others.

Mindfulness practices and creative expressions have been integrated into each chapter to provide you with tools for daily self-care and emotional balance. Mindfulness fosters a deeper connection to the present moment, while creative pursuits reconnect you with joy and personal interests. By embedding these practices into your routine, you cultivate resilience and empower yourself to navigate life's challenges with grace.

Engaging with the various reflection exercises, from journaling prompts to visualization techniques, has equipped you with valuable insights into your emotional landscape. Tracking your progress, celebrating small victories, and nurturing a supportive

community have all contributed to a well-rounded approach to personal growth. Remember, this journey is not linear; it ebbs and flows, requiring patience and kindness toward yourself as you evolve.

As you move forward, carry these lessons with you. Acknowledge that healing is an ongoing process, one that requires continued self-reflection, openness, and courage. Embrace the growth you have achieved thus far and remain committed to nurturing your authentic self. The journey to wholeness is uniquely yours—a path illuminated by the insights gained, the connections formed, and the strength discovered within.

May you embrace your authentic self with confidence, joy, and inner peace as you forge ahead into this new chapter of your life. Remember, you are not alone in this journey; countless others walk their paths of healing and self-discovery alongside you.

Celebrate your progress, honor your experiences, and cherish the possibilities that lie ahead.

Additional Thoughts and Notes

_____

_____

_____

_____

_____

_____

_____

REFERENCES

Aaron. (2024, September 8). *Master assertive communication skills for effective interpersonal interaction.* Leader Navigation. https://www.leadernavigation.com/assertive-communication-skills-2/

Ackerman, C. (2017, January 18). *22 mindfulness exercises, techniques & activities for adults.* Positive Psychology. https://positivepsychology.com/mindfulness-exercises-techniques-activities/

Ali, M. M. (2022, May 24). *The science of visualization: Can imagining your goals make you more likely to accomplish them?* Neurovine. https://www.neurovine.ai/blog/the-science-of-visualization-can-imagining-your-goals-make-you-more-likely-to-accomplish-them

Brenner, B. (2024, November 17). Understanding how trauma triggers Influence behavior and therapy options. *Therapy Group of DC.* https://therapygroupdc.com/therapist-dc-blog/understanding-how-trauma-triggers-influence-behavior-and-therapy-options/

Buchwald, N. (2023, May 11). *Embracing inner child work: Reparent and heal your inner child.* Manhattan Mental Health Counseling. https://manhattanmentalhealthcounseling.com/embracing-inner-child-work-reparent-and-heal-your-inner-child/

Center for Substance Abuse Treatment (2014). Treatment improvement protocol (TIP) series, 57, Chapter 3, Understanding the impact of trauma. In *Trauma-Informed Care in Behavioral Health Services.* Substance Abuse and Mental Health Services Administration (US). //www.ncbi.nlm.nih.gov/books/NBK207191/

charlpc4. (2024, July 8). *Progress to peace counseling & therapy services.* Progress to Peace Counseling. https://progresstopeacecounseling.com/emotional-safety-the-cornerstone-of-healthy-relationships/

Copley, L. (2024, March 29). *Reparenting: Seeking healing for your inner child.* Positive Psychology. https://positivepsychology.com/reparenting/

Cohen, J. A., & Mannarino, A. P. (2015). Trauma-focused cognitive behavior therapy for traumatized children and families. *Child and Adolescent Psychiatric Clinics of North America, 24(3):557-570.* https://doi.org/10.1016/j.chc.2015.02.005

Creating safe spaces: The importance of supportive counseling environments. (2022). Dr Beckloff. https://www.drbeckloff.com/creating-safe-spaces-the-importance-of-supportive-counseling-environments

Critcher, C. R., & Dunning, D. (2015). Self-affirmations provide a broader perspective on self-threat. *Personality & social psychology bulletin, 41*(1), 3–18. https://doi.org/10.1177/0146167214554956

Davis, A. M. B., & Carnelley, K. B. (2023, February 3). *Attachment: The what, the why, and the long-term effects.* Frontiers for Young Minds. https://doi.org/10.3389/frym.2023.809060

Field, B. (2023, November 3). *Why we self-sabotage and how to stop the cycle.* Verywell Mind. https://www.verywellmind.com/why-people-self-sabotage-and-how-to-stop-it-5207635

Finch, K., Lawrence, D., Williams, M. O., Thompson, A. R., & Hartwright, C. (2024, June 12). Relationships between adverse childhood experiences, attachment, resilience, psychological distress and trauma among forensic mental health populations. *The Journal of Forensic Psychiatry & Psychology, 35*(5): 660-684. https://doi.org/10.1080/14789949.2024.2365149

Gillis, K. (2024, September 13). *The impact of childhood trauma on adult relationships.* Psychology Today. https://www.psychologytoday.com/us/blog/invisible-bruises/202407/the-impact-of-childhood-trauma-on-adult-relationships

Godreau, J. (2024, February 16). *Emotional triggers: Why they matter & how to manage them effectively.* Mindful Health Solutions. https://mindfulhealthsolutions.com/emotional-triggers-why-they-matter-how-to-manage-them-effectively/

Goldstein, E. (n.d.). *What is an inner child & what does it know?* Integrative Psychotherapy. https://integrativepsych.co/new-blog/what-is-an-inner-child

Harvard Health. (2025, January 16). *Benefits of mindfulness.* HelpGuide.org. https://www.helpguide.org/mental-health/stress/benefits-of-mindfulness

Hirschfeld, M. (2023, March 31). *Healing your inner child: A journey of self-discovery, growth, and embracing positive narratives.* Holding Hope Marriage and Family Therapy. https://holdinghopemft.com/healing-your-inner-child/

How you can care for yourself by setting healthy boundaries. (2023, November 21). See Beyond. https://www.seebeyond.cc/blog/2023/10/25/how-you-can-care-for-yourself-by-setting-healthy-boundaries

The impact of positive relationships on mental health and well-being. (2023, October 16). Child Focus. https://www.child-focus.org/news/the-impact-of-positive-relationships-on-mental-health-and-well-being/

ImPossible Psychological Services. (2024, September 13). *Transforming negative self-talk into positive affirmations.* https://www.impossiblepsychservices.com.sg/our-resources/articles/2024/09/13/transforming-negative-self-talk-into-positive-affirmations

Lee, M. (2023, August 2). *Adverse childhood experiences: Navigating the impact on adult life.* NCACIA Protection. https://www.ncacia.org/post/adverse-childhood-experiences-navigating-the-impact-on-adult-life

Lee-Hawkins, Y. (2024, September 18). *Self-Awareness: Understanding Triggers and Stressors.* Medium. https://medium.com/@yvonneleehawkins/self-awareness-understanding-triggers-and-stressors-e9c99ad18e11

Matejko, S. (2021, July 26). *How to create emotional safety in a relationship: 7 tips.* Psych Central. https://psychcentral.com/blog/how-do-you-create-emotional-safety-in-your-relationships

Mayo Clinic Staff. (2022, October 11). *Mindfulness exercises.* Mayo Clinic. https://www.mayoclinic.org/healthy-lifestyle/consumer-health/in-depth/mindfulness-exercises/art-20046356

McCullough, M. E., & Worthington, E. L., Jr. (1995). Promoting forgiveness: The comparison of two brief psychoeducational interventions with a waiting-list control. *Counseling and Values, 40,* 55–68. http://dx.doi.org/10.1002/j.2161-007X.1995.tb00387.x

Meet your inner child. (2024, September 16). Cleveland Clinic. https://health.clevelandclinic.org/inner-child

Mindfulness for your health. (2021, June). NIH News in Health. https://newsinhealth.nih.gov/2021/06/mindfulness-your-health

Nash, J. (2018). *How to set healthy boundaries & build positive relationships*. Positive Psychology. https://positivepsychology.com/great-self-care-setting-healthy-boundaries/

The National Child Traumatic Stress Network. (2018). *Effects*. https://www.nctsn.org/what-is-child-trauma/trauma-types/complex-trauma/effects

Negative self-talk: 8 ways to quiet your inner critic. (2023, October 3). Calm Blog. https://www.calm.com/blog/negative-self-talk

Oswald, R. (2023, December 27). *Setting boundaries for well-being*. Mayo Clinic Health System. https://www.mayoclinichealthsystem.org/hometown-health/speaking-of-health/setting-boundaries-for-well-being

Pluut, H., & Wonders, J. (2020, December 23). *Not able to lead a healthy life when you need it the most: Dual role of lifestyle behaviors in the association of blurred work-life boundaries with well-being*. Frontiers in Psychology. https://doi.org/10.3389/fpsyg.2020.607294

Puff, R. (2025, January 13). *The power of self-forgiveness*. Psychology Today. https://www.psychologytoday.com/intl/blog/meditation-for-modern-life/202501/the-power-of-self-forgiveness

Rcademy Editor. (n.d.). *Boundary setting in communication: 5 ways to say no with respect*. RCademy. https://rcademy.com/boundary-setting-in-communication/

Raypole, C. (2020, July 8). *8 tips for healing your inner child*. Healthline. https://www.healthline.com/health/mental-health/inner-child-healing

Robinson, L., Segal, J., & Jaffe, J. (2024, June 20). *Attachment styles and how they affect adult relationships*. HelpGuide.org. https://www.helpguide.org/relationships/social-connection/attachment-and-adult-relationships

Saranya (n.d.). *Do you have an anxious attachment style?* Lemon8-App. https://www.lemon8-app.com/saranya222/7224186254361985542?region=us

Schultz, J. (2020, September 24). *Forgiveness in therapy: Help clients forgive themselves and others*. Positive Psychology. https://positivepsychology.com/forgiveness-in-therapy/

Sciandra, F. (2024, May 3). *100 inner child journal prompts: Reparenting for healing and growth*. https://francescasciandra.com/blog/100-inner-child-journal-prompts-reparenting-for-healing-and-growth

Smith, S. (2019, January 22). *How adult relationships can be affected by childhood*. https://suntiasmith.com/2019/01/22/how-your-childhood-affects-your-adult-relationships/

Spencer-Milnes, X. (2020, December 2). *ABC chart for challenging behaviour: Free template*. High Speed Training. https://www.highspeedtraining.co.uk/hub/abc-chart-for-challenging-behaviour/

Springer, K. W., Sheridan, J., Kuo, D., & Carnes, M. (2003). The long-term health outcomes of childhood abuse. An overview and a call to action. *Journal of General Internal Medicine*, *18*(10), 864–870. https://doi.org/10.1046/j.1525-1497.2003.20918.x

Strong relationships, strong health. (2022, February 24). Better Health Channel. https://www.betterhealth.vic.gov.au/health/HealthyLiving/Strong-relationships-strong-health

Strategies to overcome self sabotage and boost productivity. (2024, September 9). Coachup.sg. https://coachup.sg/blog-post-strategies-to-overcome-self-sabotage-and-boost-productivity/

Sweety S. (2023, April 17). *How to use accountability and support to stay motivated and achieve your goals*. Medium; Justly Blog. https://medium.com/justly/how-to-use-accountability-and-support-to-stay-motivated-and-achieve-your-goals-e4ea6edbb290

Sutton, J. (2022, October 8). *Inner child healing: 35 practical tools for growing beyond your past.* Positive Psychology. https://positivepsychology.com/inner-child-healing/

Top inner child work exercises. (2024). My People Patterns. https://www.mypeoplepatterns.com/blog/inner-child-work-exercises

Jones, R. (2023, November). 25 positive affirmations to heal childhood trauma. A Solution B. https://www.asolutionb.com/chat-trap-blog/positive-affirmations-to-heal-childhood-trauma

Understanding emotional triggers (2025, January 13). Kids First. https://www.kidsfirstservices.com/first-insights/understanding-emotional-triggers

Visualization meditation: 8 exercises to add to your practice. (2023, August 22). Calm Blog. https://www.calm.com/blog/visualization-meditation

Visualizing success: The power of mental imagery in mindset shifts. (2023, July 12). Life Coach Training and Certification. https://lifecoachtraining.co/visualizing-success-the-power-of-mental-imagery-in-mindset-shifts/

Wade, N. G., Hoyt, W. T., Kidwell, J. E. M., & Worthington, E. L., Jr. (2014). Efficacy of psychotherapeutic interventions to promote forgiveness: A meta-analysis. *Journal of Consulting and Clinical Psychology, 82*(1), 154–170. https://doi.org/10.1037/a0035268

Made in the USA
Columbia, SC
17 June 2025